PIANO / VOCAL / GUITAR

CHILDREN'S SONGS

ISBN 0-634-06733-8

7777 W. BLUEMOUND RD. P.O. BOX 13819 MILWAUKEE, WI 53213

Visit Hal Leonard Online at
www.halleonard.com

CONTENTS

A-TISKET A-TASKET

Traditional

ALPHABET SONG

Traditional

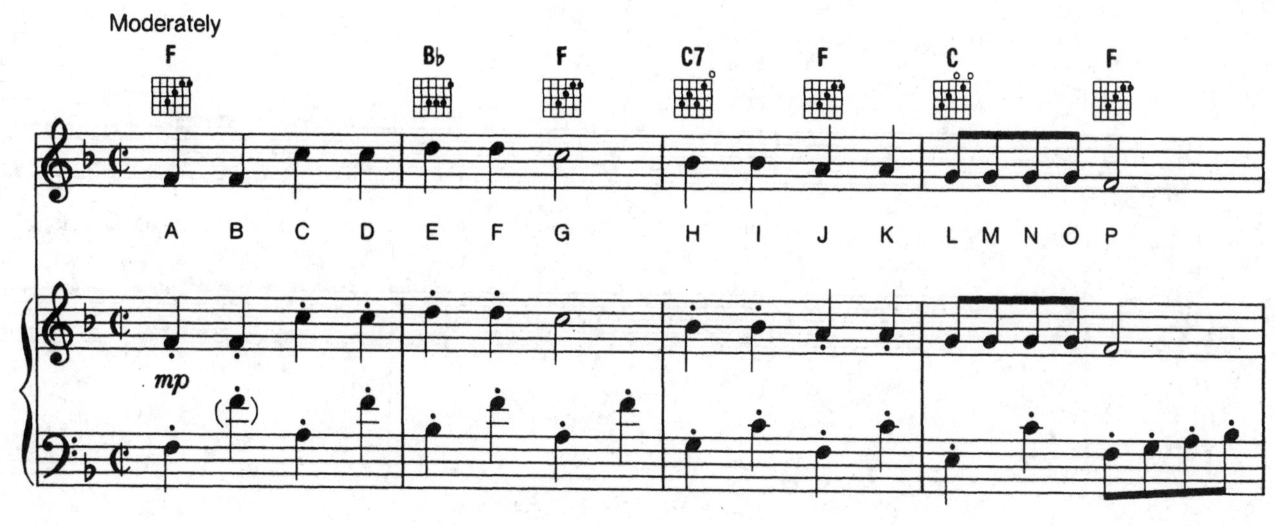

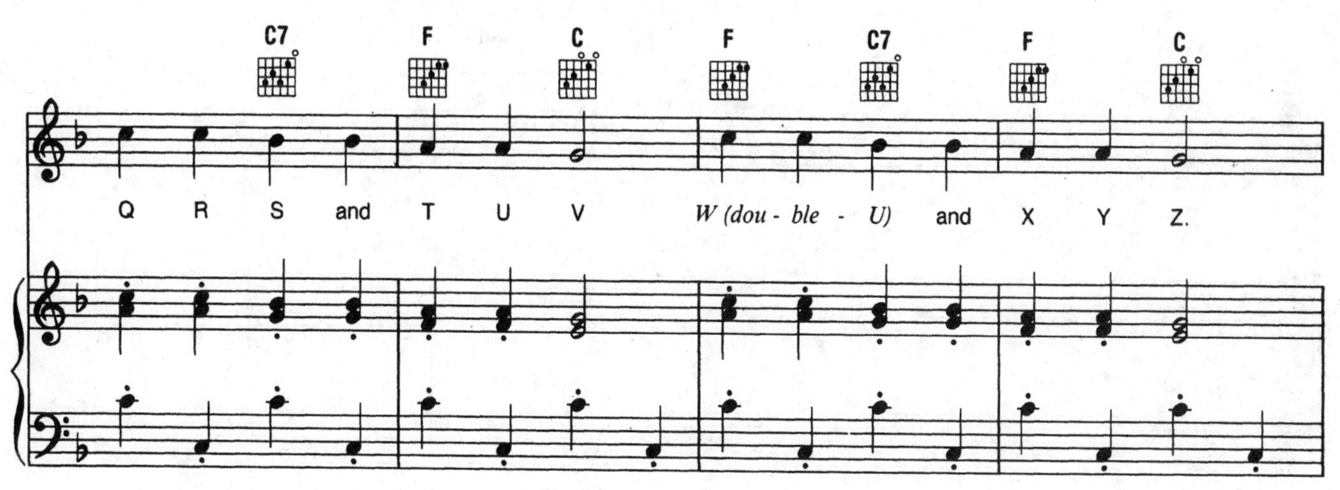

ALOUETTE

Traditional

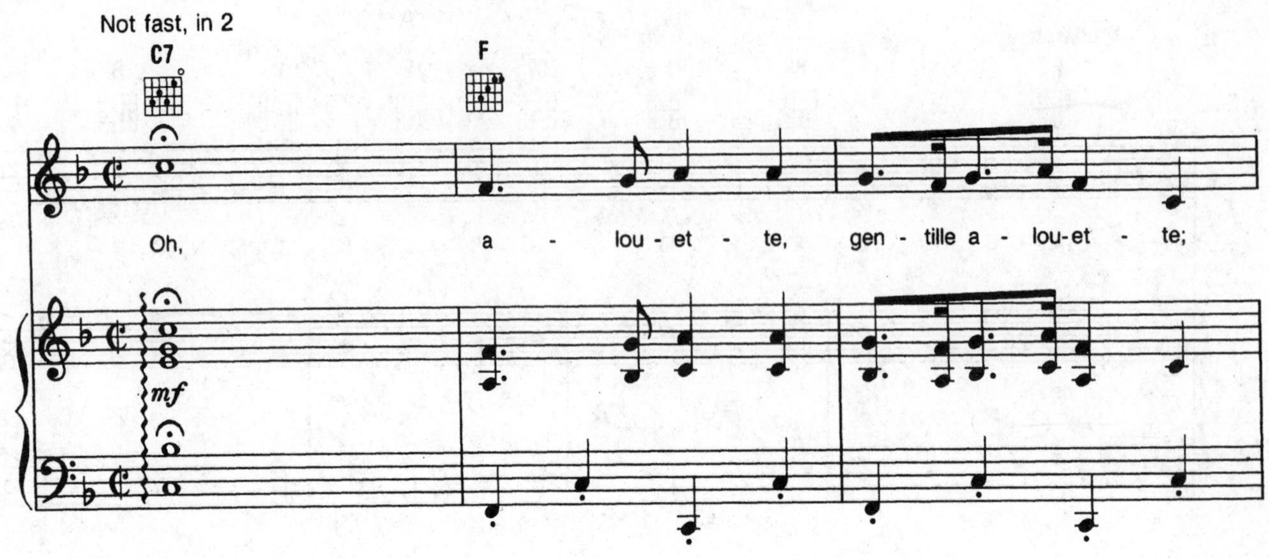

*Each chorus adds a new part of the body, in reverse order. For example, Chorus 3 is sung:

Et le nez, et le nez,
Et le bec, et le bec,
Et la têt', et le têt',
Alouett', Alouett'.
Oh, *etc.*

2. le bec *(beak)*
3. le nez *(nose)*
4. les yeux *(eyes)*
5. le cou *(neck)*
6. les ailes *(wings)*
7. le dos *(back)*
8. les pattes *(feet)*
9. la queue *(tail)*

ANIMAL CRACKERS IN MY SOUP

from CURLY TOP

Lyrics by TED KOEHLER and IRVING CAESAR
Music by RAY HENDERSON

Happily, with a bounce

B♭ Cm7 F7 B♭

An - i - mal crack - ers in my soup, mon - keys and rab - bits

mf
slightly detached

Cm F Cm/E♭ B♭/D Cm7 F7 B♭/D Cm/E♭ B♭/D

loop the loop. Gosh, oh gee, but I have fun swal - low - ing an - i - mals

Cm7 Fsus F B♭ Cm7 F7

one by one. In ev - 'ry bowl of soup I see

B♭
Cm7
F
Cm/E♭
B♭/D
Cm7
F7
B♭/D
li - ons and ti - gers watch - ing me. I make 'em jump right through a hoop, those
C♯dim7
B♭/D
Cm/E♭
Dm/F
B♭
E♭
B♭7/F
an - i - mal crack - ers in my soup. When I get hold of the
E♭/G
B♭7/F
E♭
B♭7
E♭6
D7
big bad wolf, I just push him un - der to drown. Then
Gm
D7/A
Gm/B♭
D7/A
Gm
F/A
E♭/G
Dm/F
I bite him in a mil - lion bits and I gob - ble him right

G♭7♭5
F7
B♭
Cm7
3 fr
F7
down.
When they're in - side me where it's dark,
B♭
Cm
3 fr
F
B♭/D
F7
I walk a - round like No - ah's ark.
I stuff my tum - my
To Coda
B♭
F/A
Gm
3 fr
B♭/D
Cm/E♭
3 fr
B♭/D
C7
F7
B♭
like a "goop" with an - i - mal crack - ers in my soup!
C
G/C
C
G/C
C
An - i - mal crack - ers in my soup do fun - ny things to me.

G/C
C
F/C
They make me think my neigh - bor - hood is a big men - ag - er -
C
Dm
A7/D
Dm
ie. For in - stance, there's our jan - i - tor. His
molto accel.
a tempo
A7/D
Dm
D7
Gm/D
name is Mis - ter Klein. And when he hol - lers at us kids, he re -
Faster, rollicky
A7/D
Dm
E♭
3 fr
B♭/F
minds me of a lion.

E♭/G
B♭7/A♭
E♭/B♭
B♭dim7
B♭7
E♭
The gro - cer is so
big and fat, he has a big mous - tache. He
looks just like a wal - rus just be - fore he takes a splash!
D.C. al Coda
F7
CODA
Cm/E♭
B♭/D
C7
B♭
B♭7/F
an - i - mal crack - ers in my soup!

Eb/G
Bb7/F
Eb
Bb7
Eb6
D7
Gm
D7/A
Gm/Bb
D7/A
Gm
F/A
Eb/G
Dm/F
Gb7b5
F7
Bb
When they're in - side me
Cm7
F7
Bb
Cm
F
where it's dark,
I walk a - round like
No - ah's ark.
I
Bb
F7
Bb
F/A
Gm
Bb/D
Cm/Eb
Bb/D
C7
F7
Bb
stuff my tum - my like a "goop" with an - i - mal crack - ers in my soup!

ANIMAL FAIR

American Folksong

C
C(add9)
comb - ing his au - burn hair. You ought to have seen the
Em7
Fmaj7
monk, he jumped on the el - e - phant's trunk. The el - e - phant sneezed and
Repeat ad lib
Em7
Fmaj7
G7
C
G7
C
G7
C
G7
C
G7
fell on his knees, and what be - came of the monk, the monk, the monk, the monk, the
C
Guitar Tacet
G7
C
p sub.
monk? The monk?
p sub.

ANY DREAM WILL DO

from JOSEPH AND THE AMAZING TECHNICOLOR DREAMCOAT

Music by ANDREW LLOYD WEBBER
Lyrics by TIM RICE

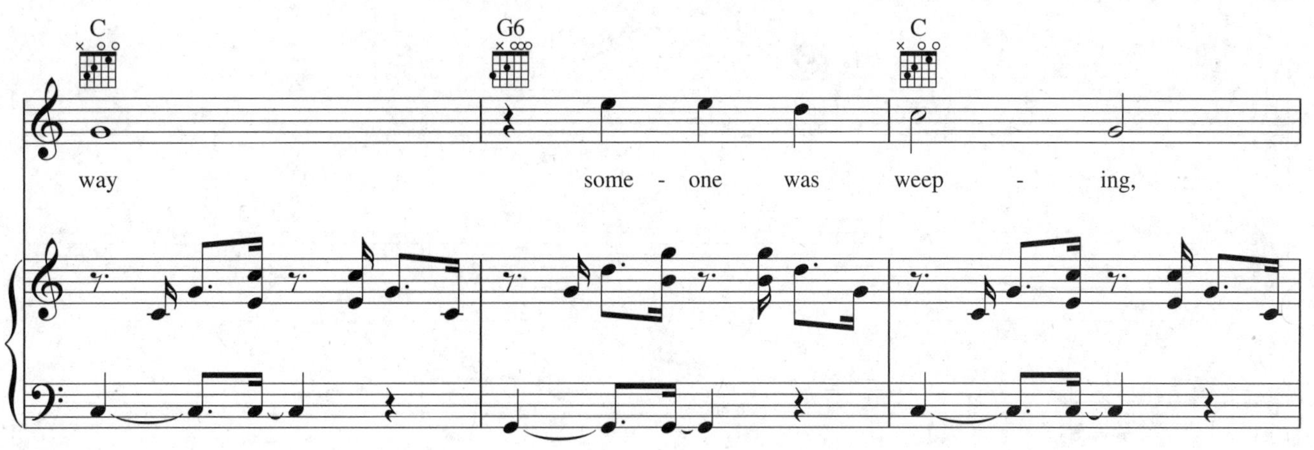
C
G6
C
way
some - one was weep - ing,

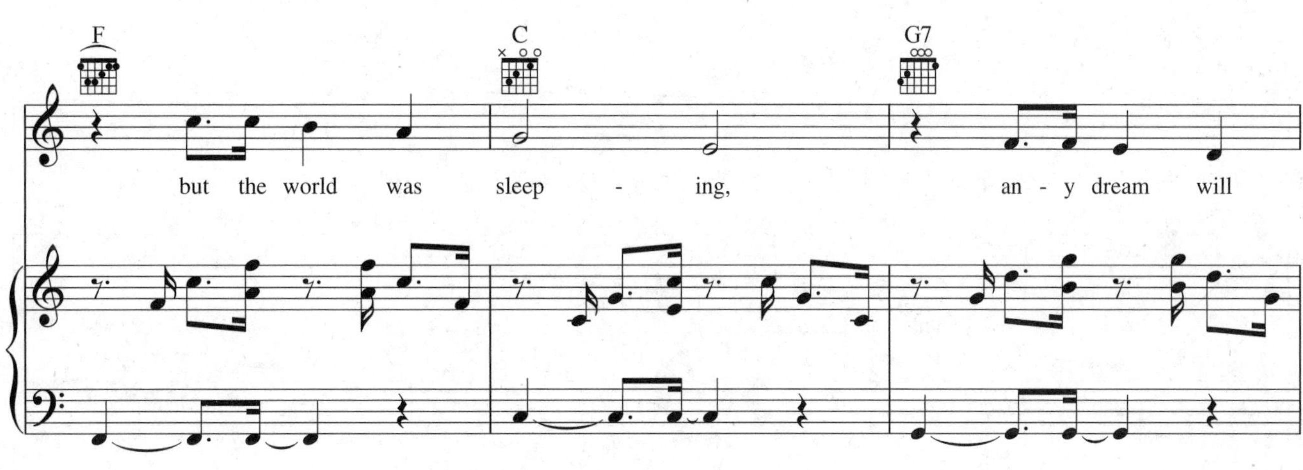
F
C
G7
but the world was sleep - ing,
an - y dream will

C
G6
G7
C
do.
I wore my coat
CHOIR:
I wore my

G6
C
F
with gold - en lin - ing, bright col - ours
coat,
ah,
C
G7
C
shin - ing won - der - ful and new.
ah,
G6
G7
C
G6
And in the east the dawn was
and in the east,

C
F
C
break - ing,
and the world was wak - ing,
ah,
ah,
G7
C
B♭/C
C7
JOSEPH:
an - y dream will do.
A
F
F6
Fmaj7
F6
D7
D
crash of drums a flash of light, my gold - en coat flew

D9
C/G G C G7 C/G G7 C/G G Dm/G G D7/G
out of sight. The colours faded into darkness, I was left a-
CHOIR:
The colours faded into darkness, ah,
G Dm7/G G7 C
lone. May I re-turn,
ah, ah. May I re-
G6 C F
to the be-gin-ning, the light is
turn, ah,

C
G7
C
dim - ming
and the dream is
too,
ah.
G6
G7
C
G6
the world and
I,
we are still
The world and
I,
C
F
C
wait - ing,
still hes - i - tat - ing
ah,
ah.

G
C
Dm7/C
an - y dream will do,
An - y dream,
an - y dream will,
C
Dm7/C
C
an - y dream will do,
an - y dream,
an - y dream will,
do,
an - y dream,
Dm7/C
C
Dm/G
C
an - y dream will do.
an - y dream will,
an - y dream,
an - y dream will do.
rall.

THE BALLAD OF DAVY CROCKETT

from Walt Disney's DAVY CROCKETT

Words by TOM BLACKBURN
Music by GEORGE BRUNS

Moderately

mf

F

F Bb F C7 F

1. Born on a moun - tain top in Ten - nes - see, Green - est state in the
2. eigh - teen - thir - teen the Creeks up - rose, addin' redskin arrows to the
3. Off through the woods _ he's a marchin' a - long, makin' up yarns an' a -

4.-10. *(See additional lyrics)*

G7 C7 F F/A Bb Gm

Land of the Free, Raised in the woods so's he knew ev - 'ry tree,
coun - try's ___ woes. Now, In - jun fightin' is some - thin' he knows, so he
sing - in' a song, itch - in' fer fightin' an' right - in' a wrong, He's

C7 F

kilt him a b'ar when he was on - ly three. Da - vy,
should - ers his rifle an' off he ___ goes. Da - vy,
ringy as a b'ar an' twict as ___ strong. Da - vy,

1-9
10
B♭ F C7 F F
Da - vy Crock-ett, King of the wild fron - tier! 2. In fear!
Da - vy Crock-ett, man who _ don't know fear!
Da - vy Crock-ett, buck - skin _ buc - ca - neer!
F C7 F B♭ F C7 F G7 C7
11.-17. (See additional lyrics)
18. he come home his pol - i - tick-in' done, The west - ern march had just be - gun, So he
19. heard of Houston an' Au-stin an' so, To the Texas plains he jest had to go, Where
20. land is biggest an' his land is best, From grass - y plains to the moun - tain _ crest, He's a -
F F/A B♭ Gm C7 F
3fr
packed his gear an' his trust - y gun, An' lit out grin-nin' to fol - low the sun.
Free - dom was fight - in' an - oth - er foe, An' they needed him at the A - la - mo.
head of us all meetin' the test, Follow - in' his leg-end in - to the West.
11-19
20
B♭ F C7 F F
clear! 18. When
Da - vy, Da - vy Crock - ett, lead - in' the pi - o - neer! 19. He
Da - vy, Da - vy Crock - ett, the man who _ don't know fear! 20. His
Da - vy, Da - vy Crock - ett, King of the wild fron - tier!

Additional Lyrics

4. Andy Jackson is our gen'ral's name,
His reg'lar soldiers we'll put to shame,
Them redskin varmints us Volunteers'll tame,
'Cause we got the guns with the sure-fire aim.
Davy - Davy Crockett,
The champion of us all!

5. Headed back to war from the ol' home place,
But Red Stick was leadin' a merry chase,
Fightin' an' burnin' at a devil's pace
South to the swamps on the Florida Trace.
Davy - Davy Crockett,
Trackin' the redskins down!

6. Fought single-handed through the Injun War
Till the Creeks was whipped an' peace was in store,
An' while he was handlin' this risky chore,
Made hisself a legend for evermore.
Davy - Davy Crockett,
King of the wild frontier!

7. He give his word an' he give his hand
That his Injun friends could keep their land,
An' the rest of his life he took the stand
That justice was due every redskin band.
Davy - Davy Crockett,
Holdin' his promise dear!

8. Home fer the winter with his family,
Happy as squirrels in the ol' gum tree,
Bein' the father he wanted to be,
Close to his boys as the pod an' the pea.
Davy - Davy Crockett,
Holdin' his young 'uns dear!

9. But the ice went out an' the warm winds came
An' the meltin' snow showed tracks of game,
An' the flowers of Spring filled the woods with flame,
An' all of a sudden life got too tame.
Davy - Davy Crockett,
Headin' on West again!

10. Off through the woods we're ridin' along,
Makin' up yarns an' singin' a song,
He's ringy as a b'ar an twice as strong,
An' knows he's right 'cause he ain't often wrong.
Davy - Davy Crockett,
The man who don't know fear!

11. Lookin' fer a place where the air smells clean,
Where the tree is tall an' the grass is green,
Where the fish is fat in an untouched stream,
An' the teemin' woods is a hunter's dream.
Davy - Davy Crockett,
Lookin' fer Paradise!

12. Now he'd lost his love an' his grief was gall,
In his heart he wanted to leave it all,
An' lose himself in the forests tall,
But he answered instead his country's call.
Davy - Davy Crockett,
Beginnin' his campaign!

13. Needin' his help they didn't vote blind,
They put in Davy 'cause he was their kind,
Sent up to Nashville the best they could find,
A fightin' spirit an' a thinkin' mind.
Davy - Davy Crockett,
Choice of the whole frontier!

14. The votes were counted an' he won hands down,
So they sent him off to Washin'ton town
With his best dress suit still his buckskins brown,
A livin' legend of growin' renown.
Davy - Davy Crockett,
The Canebrake Congressman!

15. He went off to Congress an' served a spell,
Fixin' up the Gover'ment an' laws as well,
Took over Washin'ton so we heered tell
An' patched up the crack in the Liberty Bell.
Davy - Davy Crockett,
Seein' his duty clear!

16. Him an' his jokes travelled all through the land,
An' his speeches made him friends to beat the band,
His politickin' was their favorite brand
An' everyone wanted to shake his hand.
Davy - Davy Crockett,
Helpin' his legend grow!

17. He knew when he spoke he sounded the knell
Of his hopes for White House an' fame as well,
But he spoke out strong so hist'ry books tell
An patched up the crack in the Liberty Bell.
Davy - Davy Crockett,
Seein' his duty clear!

ARKY, ARKY

Traditional

Additional Lyrics

2. The Lord told Noah to build him an arky, arky,
   Lord told Noah to build him an arky, arky,
   Build it out of gopher barky, barky,
   Children of the Lord.
   Chorus

3. The animals, the animals, they came in by twosies, twosies,
   Animals, the animals, they came in by twosies, twosies,
   Elephants and kangaroosies, roosies,
   Children of the Lord.
   Chorus

4. It rained and poured for forty daysies, daysies,
   Rained and poured for forty daysies, daysies,
   Almost drove those animals crazies, crazies,
   Children of the Lord.
   Chorus

5. The sun came out and dried up the landy, landy,
   (Look, there's the sun!) It dried up the landy, landy,
   Everything was fine and dandy, dandy,
   Children of the Lord.
   Chorus

THE BARE NECESSITIES

from Walt Disney's THE JUNGLE BOOK

Words and Music by
TERRY GILKYSON

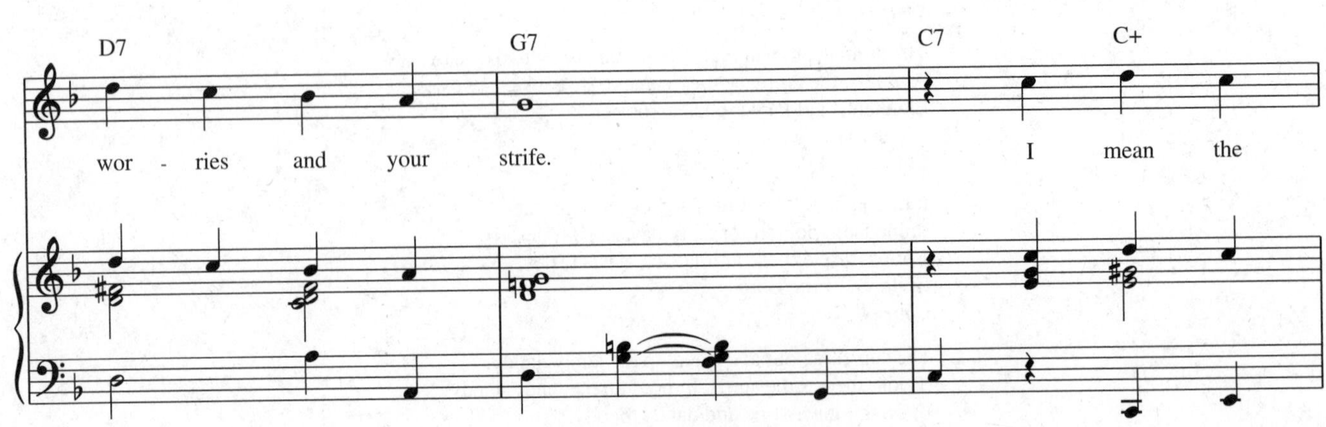

F
F7
B♭
B♭maj7
bare ne - ces - si - ties or Moth - er Na - ture's
B♭7
F
D7
G7
C7
re - ci - pes that bring the bare ne - ces - si - ties of
F
C7
life. Wher - ev - er I wan - der,
F
wher - ev - er I roam I could - n't be

C7
F
F7
fond - er of my big home. The bees are
B♭
B♭m
F
buzz - in' in the tree to make some hon - ey just for
G7
Gm7
D7
Gm7
C7
me, the bare ne - ces - si - ties of life will come to
1
F
2
F
you. Look for the you.
f

BE KIND TO YOUR WEB-FOOTED FRIENDS

Traditional

March

N.C.

mf

G

Be kind to your web - foot - ed friends, for a

D7

duck may be some - bod - y's moth - er. You

G

may think that this is the end, and it is.

BE OUR GUEST

from Walt Disney's BEAUTY AND THE BEAST

Lyrics by HOWARD ASHMAN
Music by ALAN MENKEN

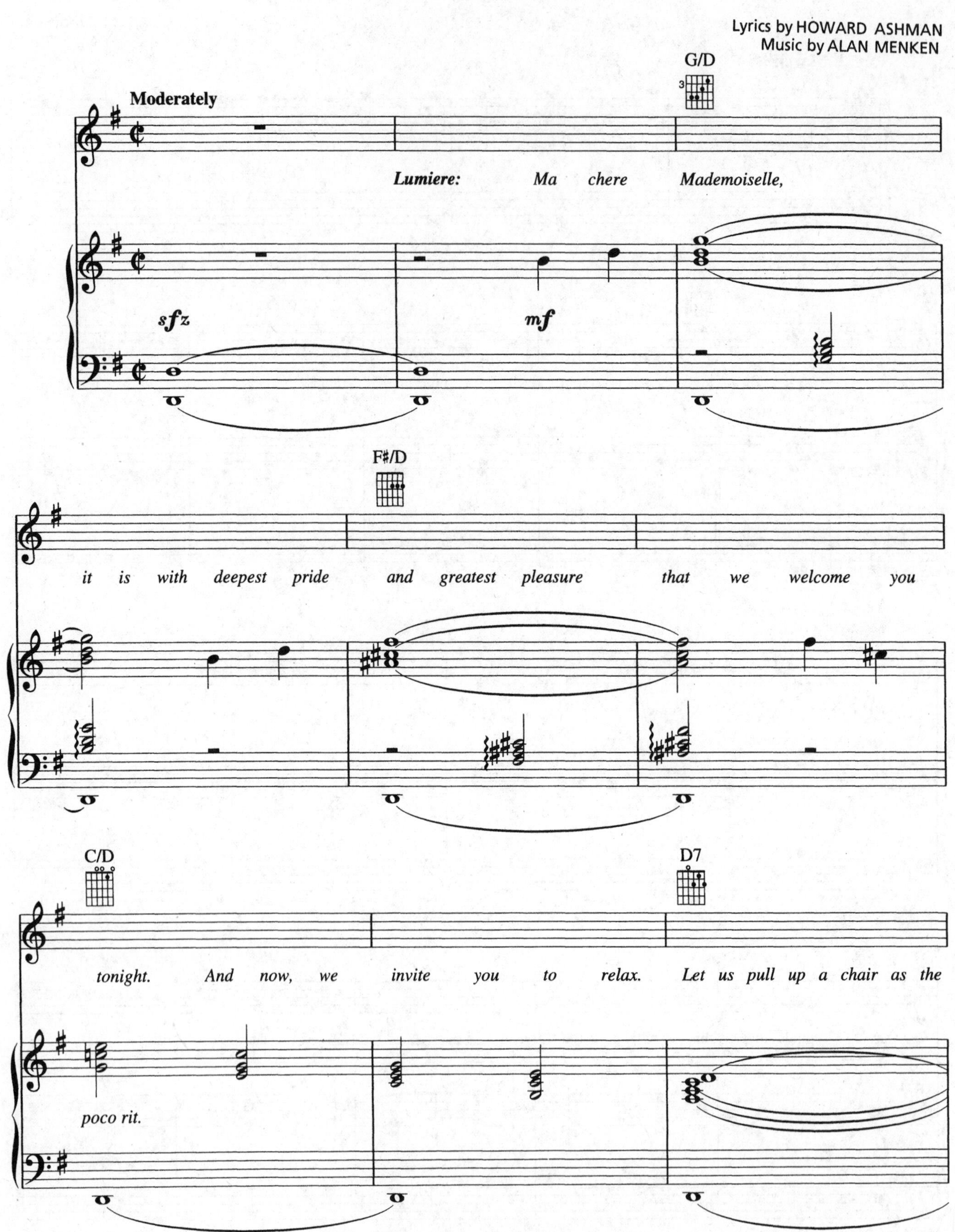

Moderate tempo
G
no chord
dining room proudly presents - your dinner!
Be our guest! Be our
Gmaj7
G6
G
guest! Put our ser - vice to the test. Tie your
G♯dim
Am7
nap - kin 'round your neck, che - rie and we pro - vide the
D7
Am
Am(♯7)
rest. Soup du jour! Hot hors d'oeuvres! Why, we

Am7
D9
Am7
on - ly live to serve. Try the grey stuff, it's de -
A#dim
Bm7
B♭9#11
Dsus/A
D7
li - cious! Don't be - lieve me? Ask the dish - es! They can
G
Gmaj7
G6
G
sing! They can dance! Af - ter all, Miss, this is France! And a
G
Gmaj7
G7
C6
din-ner here is nev - er sec-ond best. Go on, un -

B
C#m7
Ddim
B7/D#
E11
A7
fold your men - u, take a glance, and then you'll be our
Am7
D7
G
Eb7
Db/F
Eb/G
guest, oui, our guest! Be our guest! Beef ra -
Ab
Abmaj7
Ab6
Ab
gout! Cheese souf - flé! Pie and pud - ding "en flam - bé!" We'll pre -
Adim
Bbm7
pare and serve with flair a cu - li - na - ry ca - ba -

E♭7
B♭m
B♭m♯7
ret. You're a - lone and you're scared but the
B♭m7
E♭9
B♭m7
ban - quet's all pre - pared. No - one's gloom - y or com -
Bdim
Cm7
Bm7♭5
B♭m7
E♭7
plain - ing while the flat - ware's en - ter - tain - ing. We tell
A♭
A♭maj7
A♭6
A♭
jokes. I do tricks with my fel - low can - dle - sticks. Mugs: And it's

A♭maj7
A♭7
D♭6
all in per - fect taste. That you can bet! All: Come on and
C
B♭/D
E♭dim
C7/E
Fm7
lift your glass. You've won your own free pass
B♭7
B♭m7
E♭7
to be our guest! Lumiere: If you're stressed, it's fine
Cm7
F7
B♭m7
din - ing we sug - gest. All: Be our guest! Be our
f

Slower, melancholy
Db/Eb
Eb7
Ab
C
Fm
guest! Be our guest!
Lumiere: Life is so un -
mp freely
C/E
nerv - ing for a ser - vant who's not serv - ing. He's not
Ebdim
Bb/D
whole with - out a soul to wait up - on.
Dbdim
Cm7
Ah, those good old days when we were use - ful.

Fm7
B♭m7
C7sus
Sud-den - ly, those good old days are gone.
C7
Fm
C/E
Ten years, we've been rust - ing, need - ing so much more than
melodramatically
E♭dim
3
dust - ing. Need - ing ex - er - cise, a chance to use our
B♭sus4/D
B♭/D
D♭dim
skills. Most days, we just lay a - round the

A tempo
Cm7
Fm7
B♭m7
cas - tle.
Flab - by, fat and
E♭7
E7
Mrs. Potts:
laz - y. You walked in,
and oops - a - dai - sy!
It's a
A
Amaj7
A6
guest! It's a guest!
Sakes a - live, well, I'll be
A
A♯dim
blessed!
Wine's been poured and thank the Lord I've had the

Bm7
E9
Bm
Bm#7
nap - kins fresh - ly pressed. With des - sert she'll want tea. And my
Bm7
E9
Bm7
dear, that's fine with me. While the cups do their soft
Cdim
C#m7
C7#11
Bm7
E9
shoe - ing, I'll be bub - bling! I'll be brew - ing! I'll get
A
Amaj7
A6
A
warm, pip - ing hot! Heav - en's sakes! Is that a spot? Clean it up!

Amaj7
A7
D6
We want the com - pan - y im - pressed! We've got a
C#7
B/D#
Em6
C#7/E#
F#m7
lot to do. Is it one lump or two
B7
Bm7
E13
for you, our guest, Chorus: She's our guest! Mrs. Potts: She's our
C#m7
F#13
B
guest! Chorus: She's our guest! Be our guest! Be our

Bmaj7
B6
B
guest! Our com - mand is your re - quest. It's ten
Cdim
C#m7
years since we had an - y - bod - y here, and we're ob -
F#7
C#m
C#m#7
C#m7
sessed. With your meal, with your ease, yes, in - deed, we aim to
F#7
F#7sus
F#7
please. While the can - dle - light's still glow - ing let us
molto rit.

Much slower
G7sus
G7
Em/G
G7
C
help you, we'll keep go - ing course by course, one by
Cmaj7
C6
C
one! 'Til you shout, "E - nough. I'm done!" Then we'll
accel. poco a poco
C
Cmaj7
C7
C7/E
F6
sing you off to sleep as you di - gest. To - night you'll
E
D/F#
Gdim
E7/G#
Am7
D7
prop your feet up! But for now, let's eat up! Be our

Dm
Edim
guest! Be our guest! Be our
Dm7/F
G7sus
G7
guest! Please, be our
poco rit.
C
Cmaj7
C6
C+
guest!
a tempo
C

THE BEAR WENT OVER THE MOUNTAIN

Traditional

1
2
F
B♭/F
C7
B♭
Bdim
F/C
see, ___ to see what he could see. Oh, the
side, ___ he saw the oth - er
side. Oh, the bear went o - ver the moun - tain, the
bear went o - ver the moun - tain, the bear went o - ver the
moun - tain to see what he could see.

THE BIBLE TELLS ME SO

Words and Music by
DALE EVANS

G7
C
G
en - e - mies
and the bless - ed Lord you'll sure - ly please.
D7
G
C/G
How do I know? The Bi - ble tells me so.
G
C
Don't wor - ry 'bout to - mor - row, just
G/D
A7
be real good to - day. The Lord is right be -

D7
side you, He'll guide you all the way. Have
G
D7
G7
C
faith, hope and char - i - ty; that's the way to live suc -
G
D7
cess - ful - ly. How do I know? The Bi - ble tells me
1
G
C/G
G
D7
2
G
C/D
G
so. Have so.
rall.

A BICYCLE BUILT FOR TWO
(Daisy Bell)

Words and Music by
HARRY DACRE

C7
F
I'm
half
cra
-
Dm
G7
zy
all
for
the
love
of
C7
you.
It
won't
be
a
F
C7
styl
-
ish
mar
-
riage.
I

F
B♭
F/A
can't af - ford a car - riage.
C7
F
C7
But you'll look sweet
F
C7
F
on the seat of a bi - cy - cle
C7
F
built for two.

BINGO

NOTE: Each time a letter of BINGO is deleted in the lyric, clap your hands in place of singing the letter.

Traditional

C D G D G
was a farm - er had a dog and Bin - go was his name - o.
Em Am D G C
— - I - N - G - O, — - I - N - G - O, — - I -
— - — - — - G - O, — - — - — - G - O, — - — -
— - — - — - — - —, — - — - — - — - —, — - — -
Am D7
N - G - O
— - G - O
— - — - —
and Bin - go was his name There
name - o.
1,2 C/G G
3 C/G G

THE BLUE TAIL FLY
(Jimmy Crack Corn)

Words and Music by
DANIEL DECATUR EMMETT

C7
Jim - my crack corn and I don't care,
Jim - my crack corn and
F
I don't care,
F
Jim - my crack corn and I don't care,
B♭
old
1-4
C7
F
mas - ter's gone a - way.
5
C7
2. He
3. The
4. Old
5. A
mas - ter's
F
gone a - way.
3
C7
F

BOB THE BUILDER

"Intro Theme Song"

Words and Music by
PAUL JOYCE

A♭
E♭
4fr
6fr
Scoop, Muck and Diz - zy and Ro - ley too; Lof - ty and Wen - dy
Time to get bus - y; such a lot to do, build - ing and fix - ing 'til it's
F
B♭
join the crew. Bob and the gang have so much fun
good as new. Bob and the gang make a real - ly good sound,
B♭5
E♭5
work - ing to - geth - er to get the job done.
work - ing all day 'til the sun goes down.
Bob the Build - er.
A♭5
(Can we fix it?) Bob the Build - er. (Yes, we can!)
(Spoken): I think so.

Eb5
6fr
Ab5
4fr
Bb5
6fr
Eb
6fr
Bob the Build - er. (Can we fix it?) Bob the Build - er.
Bb5
6fr
Eb5
6fr
1
Abmaj7/Eb
4fr
(Yes, we can!)
Bb5
6fr
Eb5
6fr
2
Bb7
Female: It's an ur - gent job.

E♭5
6fr
Oh, please,
Can you fix it?
G7
Cm
3fr
Male: Right!
Left a bit.
Right a lit - tle.
G7
Cm
3fr
A♭
4fr
O - kay (o - kay), straight down.
We can tack - le an - y
E♭
6fr
F7
B♭
sit - u - a - tion.
Look out; here we come.
(All right.)
Can we

Bb7
dig it? (Yes!) Can we build it? (Yes!) Can we fix it? (Yes!)
Eb5 Ab5 Bb5
(Rrr.) Bob the Build - er. (Can we fix it?)
Eb Bb5 Eb5 Eb
Bob the Build - er. (Yes, we can!) Bob the Build - er.
(Spoken:) I think so.
Ab5 Bb5 Eb Bb5 Eb5
(Can we fix it?) Bob the Build - er. (Yes, we can!)
6fr
4fr

Ab
Eb
Ab/Eb
Eb
Ab
Eb
4fr
6fr
Dig - ging and mix - ing, hav - ing so much fun, (Yeah!) work - ing to - geth - er they
Bb
Eb
C7
get the job done. Can we dig it? (Yes!) Can we build it? (Yes!) Can we
F
fix it? (Yes!) (Rrr.) Bob the Build - er.
C5
3fr
(Spoken): Yeah! Bob the Build - er. (Spoken): All together now.

F
B♭5
C5
3fr
F
Bob the Build - er. (Can we fix it?) Bob.
(Spoken): Fantastic!
B♭5
C5
3fr
F
A♭
4fr
B♭
6fr
Bob the Build - er. (Can we fix it?)
(Yes, yes, we can!)
F
A♭
4fr
B♭
F
Bob the Build - er. (Oh.) Bob the Build - er.
A♭
4fr
B♭
F
C5
3fr
F5
Can we fix it? Bob the Build - er. (Yes we can!)

CAMPTOWN RACES

Words and Music by
STEPHEN C. FOSTER

A7
D
Solo:
Oh! doo - dah - day! I come down dah wid my
Oh! doo - dah - day! De blind hoss stick - en in a
Oh! doo - dah day! Den fly a - long like a
Oh! doo - dah - day! I win my mon - ey on de
A7
Chorus:
Solo:
hat caved in. Doo - dah! Doo - dah! I
big mud - hole. Doo - dah! Doo - dah!
rail - road car. Doo - dah! Doo - dah!
bob - tail nag. Doo - dah! Doo - dah! I
D
A7
D
Chorus:
go back home wid a pock-et full of tin. Oh! doo - dah - day!
Can't touch bot-tom wid a ten - foot _ pole. Oh! doo - dah - day!
Run - nin' a race wid a shoot - in' __ star. Oh! doo - dah - day!
keep my mon-ey in an old __ tow - bag. Oh! doo - dah - day!

Chorus:
G/D
D
Gwine to run all night! Gwine to run all day! I'll
Em/G
A7
D
bet my mon-ey on de bob-tail nag; some-bod-y bet on de bay.
Em/G
E7/G♯
A
D
A7
1-3
4
De
Old

THE BRADY BUNCH

Theme from the Paramount Television Series THE BRADY BUNCH

Words and Music by SHERWOOD SCHWARTZ
and FRANK DEVOL

D7
Am7
D7
All of them had hair of gold
They were four men liv - ing all to -
Am7
D7
1
like their moth - er, the young - est
geth - er, yet they were
G
2
one in curls. Girls: It's the all a -
G
G7
C/G
G
E♭7
A♭
4fr
lone. All: 'Til the one day when the
f
mf

A♭maj7
A♭6
3fr
A♭
4fr
la - dy met this fel - low, and they
B♭m7
knew that it was much more than a hunch
E♭
3fr
B♭m7
E♭7
that this group must some - how form a
B♭m7
E♭7
B♭m7
fam - 'ly. That's the way we all be -

Eb7
Ab
4fr
came the Bra - dy Bunch. The Bra - dy
Db
Db7
Gb/Db
Db
Ab
Ab7
Db/Ab
Ab
Bunch, the Bra - dy Bunch. That's the
Bb
Eb
3fr
Eb7
way we be - came the Bra - dy
Ab
Db/Ab
Ab
N.C.
Ab7
Bunch.
f

BUFFALO GALS
(Won't You Come Out Tonight?)

Words and Music by
COOL WHITE (JOHN HODGES)

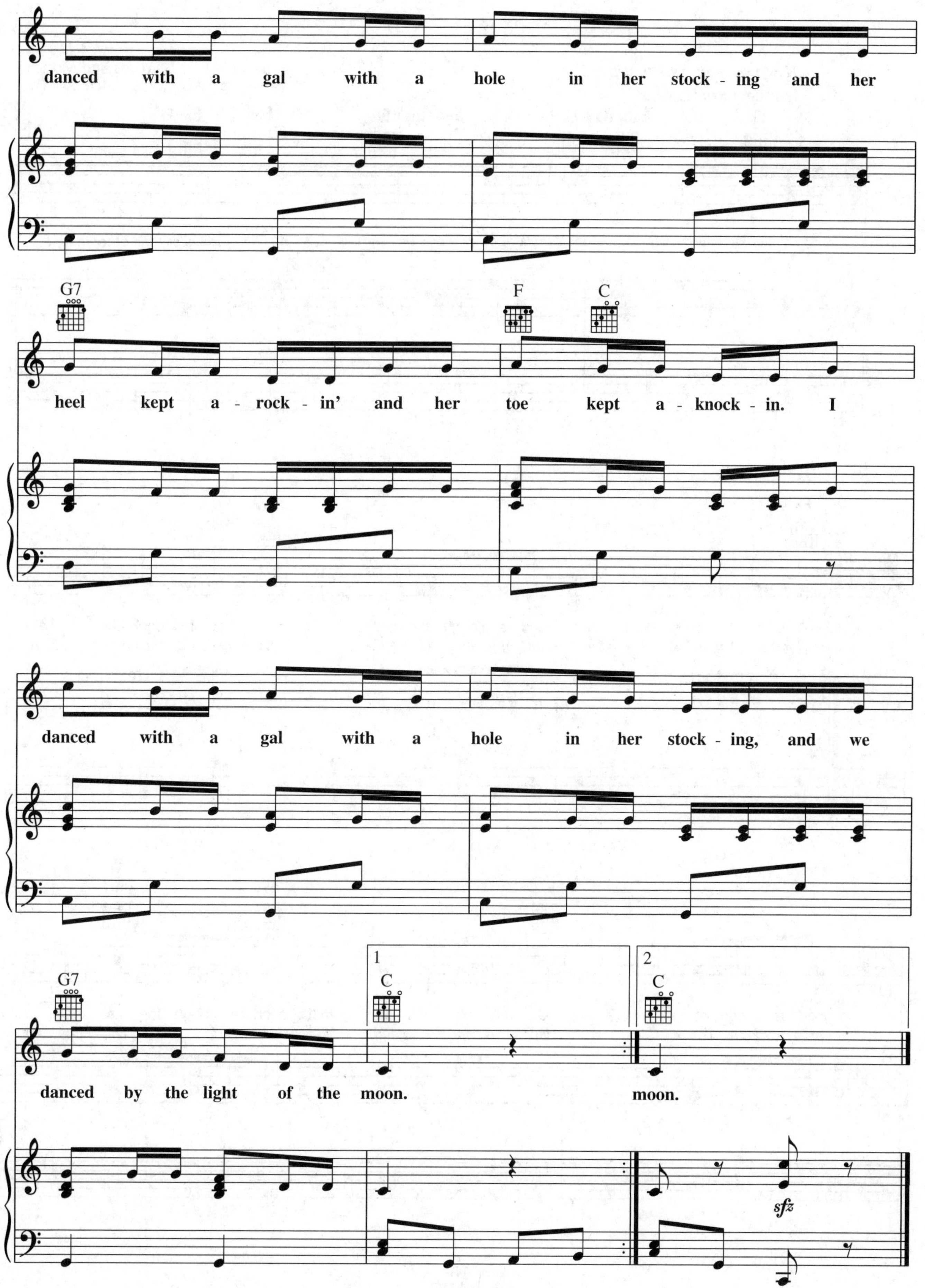
danced with a gal with a hole in her stock - ing and her
G7
F
C
heel kept a - rock - in' and her toe kept a - knock - in. I
danced with a gal with a hole in her stock - ing, and we
G7
1
C
2
C
danced by the light of the moon.
moon.
sfz

"C" IS FOR COOKIE

Words and Music by
JOE RAPOSO

Eb/Bb
Bb7
To Coda
1 Eb
no chord
2 Eb
no chord
cook - ie, cook - ie, cook - ie starts with C.
moon sometimes looks like a C,
C. (Spoken:) Hey, you know what?
3
D.S. al Coda
Eb
Bb7
no chord
but you can't eat that. So
CODA
Eb
Eb/Bb
Bb7
C. Yeah! Cook - ie, cook - ie, cook - ie starts with
Eb
Eb/Bb
Bb7
Eb
C. Oh boy! Cook - ie, cook - ie, cook - ie starts with C.

THE CANDY MAN

from WILLY WONKA AND THE CHOCOLATE FACTORY

Words and Music by LESLIE BRICUSSE
and ANTHONY NEWLEY

F7sus
F7
Fm7/B♭
E♭
Fm7/B♭
can - dy man
The can - dy man can
E♭
Cm7
F7sus
F7
Fm7/B♭
The can - dy man can 'cause he mix - es it with love and makes the
E♭
Fm7/B♭
1 E♭
Fm7/B♭
2 E♭
E♭7
world taste good.
The
A♭maj7
Adim7
E♭/B♭
can - dy man makes ev - 'ry-thing he bakes sat - is - fy - ing and de -
mf

E♭maj7
Am7♭5
D7♯5
Gm
Gm7
C7♭9
li - cious. Talk a - bout your child - hood wish - es!
Fm7
B♭7
E♭
You can e - ven eat the dish - es! Who can take to - mor - row,
mp
C7♭9
Fm7
B♭7
B♭m7
E♭9
dip it in a dream,
A♭
D♭9
E♭
Cm7
F7sus
F7
sep - a-rate the sor - row and col - lect up all the cream? The can - dy man,

Fm7/B♭
E♭
Fm7/B♭
E♭
Cm7
The can - dy man can
The
F7sus
F7
Fm7/B♭
E♭
Fm7/B♭
can - dy man can 'cause he mix - es it with love and makes the world taste good.
1 E♭
E♭7
2 E♭
Cm7
F7sus
F7
The
And the world tastes good 'cause the
Fm7/B♭
E♭
A♭
E♭
can - dy man thinks it should.

CASPER THE FRIENDLY GHOST

from the Paramount Cartoon

Words by MACK DAVID
Music by JERRY LIVINGSTON

F
C
G7
C
al - ways says "Hel - lo," and he's real - ly glad to meet cha. Wher -
F
C
D7
G7
ev - er he may go, he's kind to ev - 'ry liv - ing crea - ture.
C
C♯dim7
Grown - ups don't un - der - stand why chil - dren love him the most, but
Dm7
G7
C
Am
Dm7
G7
Cm
3fr
G7
C
kids all know that he loves them so, Cas - per the friend - ly ghost.
f
p

(Oh, My Darling)
CLEMENTINE

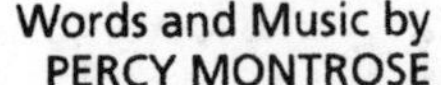

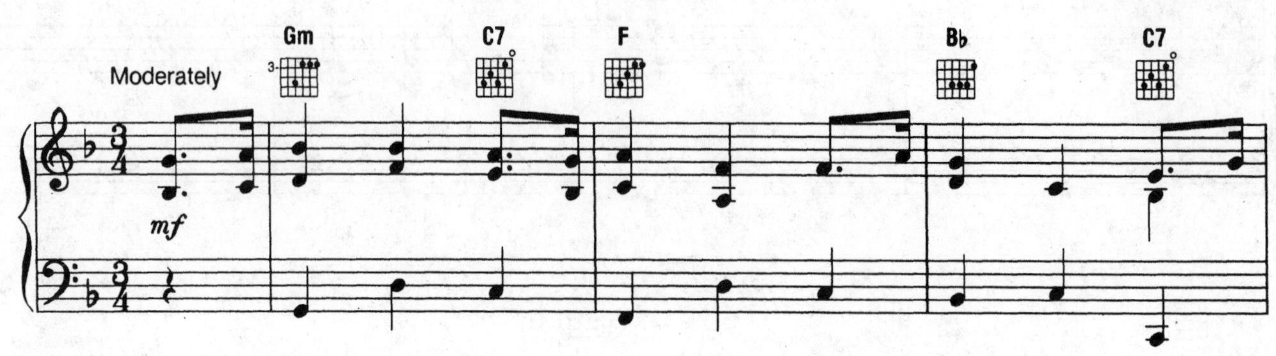

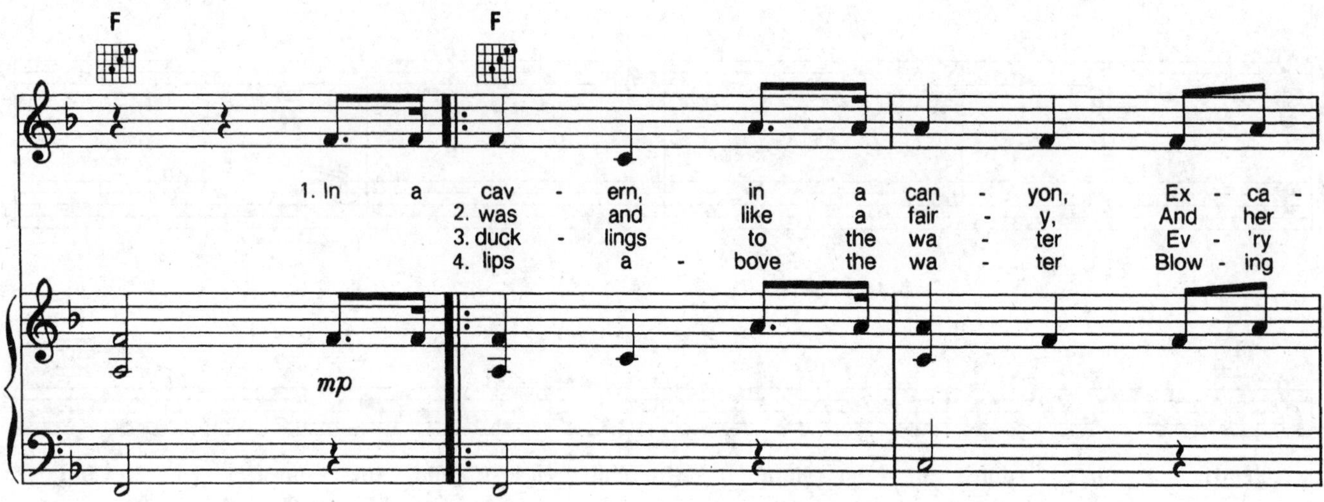

F
Dm
Gm
C7
F
nin - er, And his daugh - ter Clem - en - tine.
top - ses, San - dals were for Clem - en - tine.
splin - ter, Fell in - to the foam - ing brine.
swim - mer, So I lost my Clem - en - tine.
Oh, my
dar - ling, Oh, my dar - ling, Oh, my dar - ling Clem - en -
mf
C7
Gm7
C7
F
Dm
tine, You are lost and gone for - ev - er, Dread - ful
Gm
C7
1,2,3
F
4
F
sor - ry, Clem - en - tine.
2. Light she
3. Drove she
4. Ru - by tine.

DEEP AND WIDE

Traditional

DO LORD

Traditional

B7
Em
Cm6/E♭
G/D
D7
out - shines the sun,
you take Him too,
'way be - yond the
G
C/G
G
blue.
Do Lord, oh, do Lord, oh,
do re - mem - ber me.
C
Do Lord, oh,
do Lord, oh, do re - mem - ber me.
G

B7
Do Lord, oh, do Lord, oh, do re - mem - ber
Em
Cm6/E♭
1
G/D
D7
G
C/G
me, 'way be - yond the blue.
G
2
G/D
D7
'way be - yond
G
C/G
G
the blue.
rit.

DO-RE-MI

from THE SOUND OF MUSIC

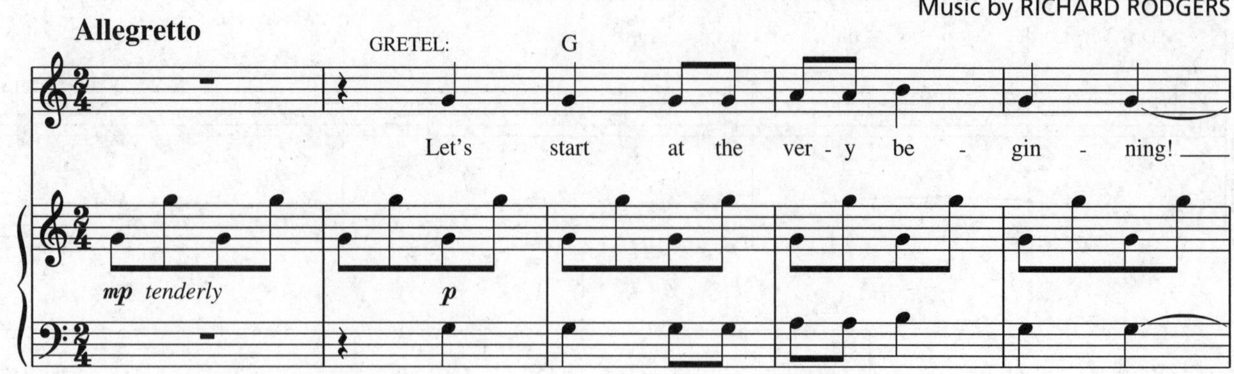

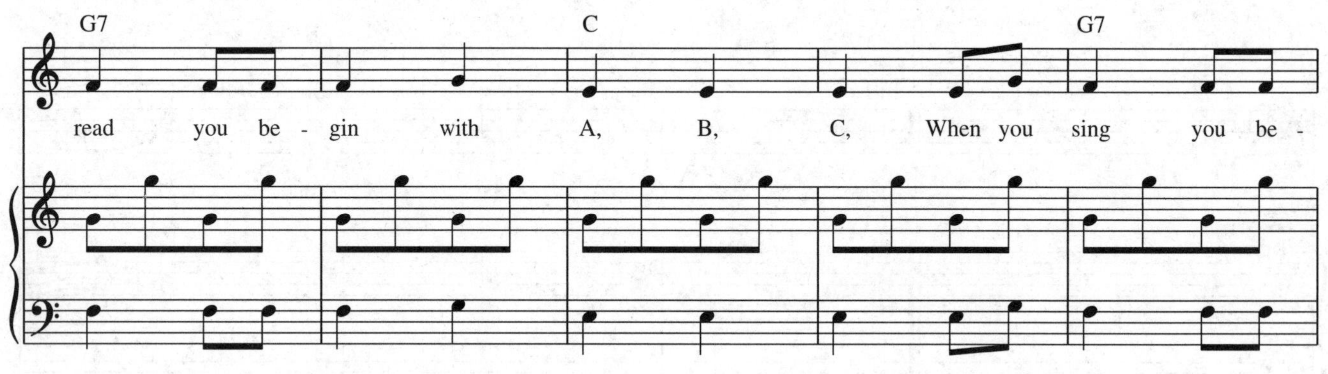

MARIA:
G
G7
C
G7
Do - re - mi. The first three notes just hap - pen to
C
G
C
CHILDREN:
G
C
be do - re - mi! Do - re - mi!
MARIA:
G7
(Spoken)
C
G7
Do - re - mi - fa - so - la - ti
All right, I'll make
it easier. Listen:
mf
Refrain (in spirited tempo)
C
MARIA:
G7
Doe a deer, a fe - male deer, Ray a drop of gold - en
mp

G9
G7
C
sun,
Me
a name I call my - self,
G9
C
C7
Far
a long, long way to run.
Sew
a nee - dle pull - ing
poco a poco cresc.
F
D7
G
thread,
La
a note to fol - low sew,
E7
Am
C7
F
Dm7
Tea
a drink with jam and bread
That will bring us
mf

G7
C
G
C
back to do - oh - oh - oh! (Guitar) A deer, a fe - male
p
CHILDREN:
(spoken)
G7
MARIA:
G9
G7
CHILDREN:
deer, Do! (Guitar) A drop of gold - en sun, Re!
C
MARIA:
CHILDREN:
G9
MARIA:
(Guitar) A name I call my - self, Mi! (Guitar) A
G9
C
C7
CHILDREN:
MARIA:
(sung)
CHILDREN:
long, long way to run, Fa! So! A nee - dle pull - ing
poco a poco cresc.

F
D7
MARIA:
CHILDREN:
G
thread.
La! A note to fol - low so!
E7
MARIA:
CHILDREN:
Am
C7
MARIA:
F
Dm7
G7
Ti! A drink with jam and bread
That will bring us back to
mf
C
ALL:
G7
Doe a deer, a fe - male deer,
Ray a drop of gold - en
mf
G9
C
sun,
Me a name I call my - self,

G9
C
C7
Far ___ a long, long way to run.
Sew ___ a nee - dle pull - ing
poco a poco cresc.
F
D7
G
thread,
La ___ a note to fol - low sew,
E7
Am
C7
F
Dm7
G7
Tea ___ a drink with jam and bread
That will bring us back to
mf
C
C7
F
F/E
Dm7
G7
C
doe!
Do - re - mi - fa - so - la - ti - do!
f

DOWN BY THE STATION

Traditional

F
row.
See the en - gine driv - er
Gm7
3 fr
C7
F
pull the lit - tle han - dle.
Choo! Choo! Toot! Toot!
Gm7
3 fr
C
F
Off they go.

DOWN IN MY HEART

Traditional

F
B♭
N.C.
down in my heart to stay! I've got the love of Je - sus, love of Je - sus
B♭
F7
B♭
N.C.
down in my heart, (Where?) down in my heart, (Where?) down in my heart. I've got the
B♭
F7
love of Je - sus, love of Je - sus down in my heart, (Where?) down in my heart to
B♭
E♭/B♭
6fr
B♭
N.C.
B♭
stay. I've got the peace that pass - eth un - der - stand - ing down in my heart, (Where?)

F
F7
B♭
N.C.
down in my heart, (Where?) down in my heart. I've got the
peace that pass-eth un-der-stand-ing down in my heart, (Where?) down in my heart to
F7
stay, down in my heart to
B♭7
E♭/B♭
E♭m6/B♭
stay!

EENSY WEENSY SPIDER

Traditional

THE FARMER IN THE DELL

Traditional

3. The wife takes a child, etc.
4. The child takes a nurse, etc.
5. The nurse takes a dog, etc.
6. The dog takes a cat, etc.
7. The cat takes a rat, etc.
8. The rat takes the cheese, etc.
9. The cheese stands alone, etc.

FRÈRE JACQUES
(Are You Sleeping?)

Traditional

FOR HE'S A JOLLY GOOD FELLOW

Traditional

B♭
F
B♭
no - bod - y can de - ny, which no - bod - y can de -
day - light does ap - pear, till day - light does ap -
F
B♭
F
ny. For he's a jol - ly good fel - low, for
pear. We won't go home un - til morn - ing, we
C7
F
F7
he's a jol - ly good fel - low. For he's a jol - ly good
won't go home un - til morn - ing. We won't go home un - til
B♭
C7
1 F
2 F
fel - low, which no - bod - y can de - ny. We
morn - ing, till day - light does ap - pear.

GIVE ME OIL IN MY LAMP

Traditional

A♭
E♭/B♭
B♭7
E♭
N.C.
burn-ing, burn-ing burn-ing, keep me burn-ing till the break of day!
seek-ing, seek-ing, seek-ing, keep us seek-ing till the break of day!
shin-ing, shin-ing, shin-ing, keep me shin-ing till the break of day!
E♭
A♭
Fm/A♭
Sing ho - san - na, sing ho - san - na,
B♭7
E♭
A♭
E♭
B♭7
E♭
sing ho - san - na to the King of kings! Sing ho - san - na
A♭
Fm/A♭
B♭7
1,2
E♭
sing ho - san - na, sing ho - san - na to the King!
Make us
Give me

3
E♭
3fr
B7
E
King!
Sing ho - san - na,
f
A
F♯m
B7
E
A
E
A/B
sing ho - san - na, sing ho - san - na to the King of kings!
E
A
F♯m
B7
Sing ho - san - na, sing ho - san - na, sing ho - san - na to the
C♯m
4fr
C7
E/B
B7
E
King! Sing ho - san - na to the King!
8vb

HAPPY TRAILS

from the Television Series THE ROY ROGERS SHOW

Words and Music by
DALE EVANS

Slow and Tenderly

E♭6

mp

Fm7 B♭7 E♭6

Some trails are

C7 Fm

hap - py ones, oth - ers are blue. It's the

B♭7

way you ride the trail that counts; here's a

E♭
3 fr
E♭
3 fr
hap - py one for you.
Hap - py trails to
Edim7
you until we meet a -
B♭7
B♭7sus
B♭7
gain.
Hap - py trails to you, keep
B♭7♯5
E♭(add9)
E♭
3 fr
smil - in' un - til then.
Who

E♭7
A♭maj7
A♭6
3fr
cares a - bout the clouds when we're to - geth - er? Just
C7
F9
B♭7
sing a song and bring the sun - ny weath - er. Hap - py
E♭
3fr
B♭m6
6fr
C7
Fm
B♭7
trails to you till we meet a -
1
E♭
3fr
B♭7
2
E♭
3fr
A♭
4fr
E♭6
gain. Hap - py gain.

THE GOSPEL TRAIN

African-American Spiritual

A
D
chil - dren, get on board, lit - tle chil - dren, get on board, lit - tle
B7
A/E
E7
A
D
chil - dren, there's room for man - y - a more. Oh, get on board, lit - tle
A
D
chil - dren, get on board, lit - tle chil - dren, get on board, lit - tle
B7
A/E
E7
1-3
A
4
A
chil - dren, there's room for man - y - a more.
I
The
She's
more.

HAKUNA MATATA

from Walt Disney Pictures' THE LION KING

Music by ELTON JOHN
Lyrics by TIM RICE

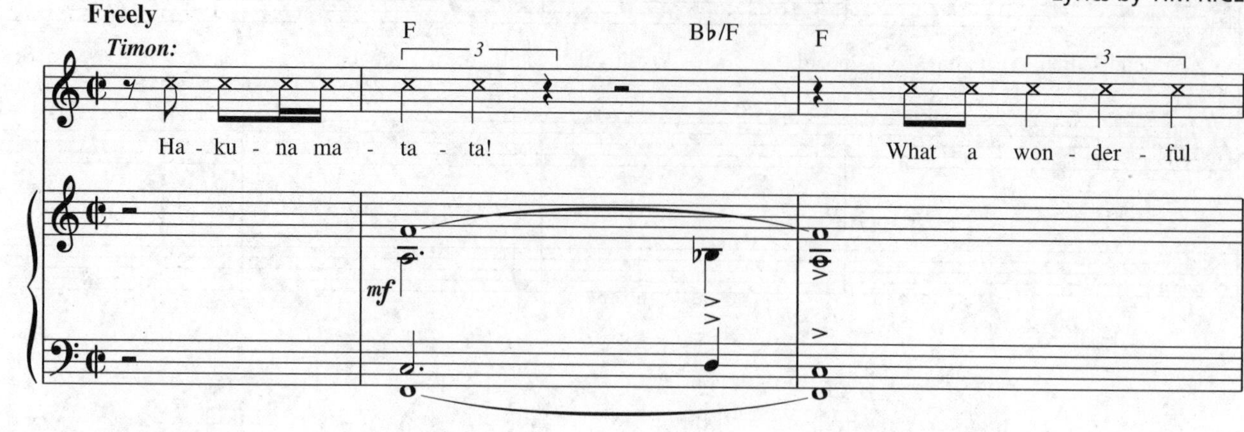

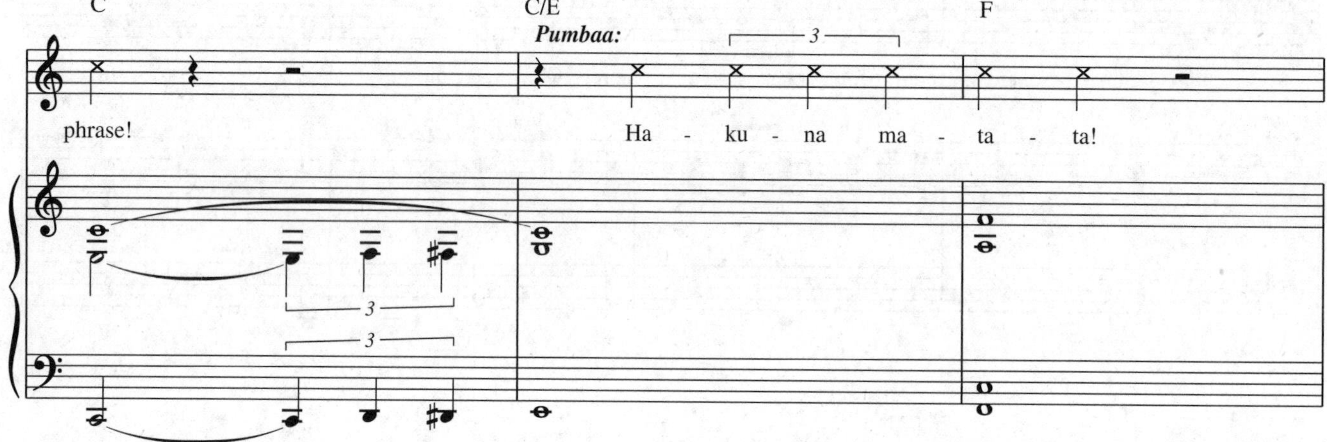

G7
Timon:
C
phi - los - o - phy.
Ha - ku - na ma - ta - ta.
B♭
F
Simba: Hakuna matata?
Pumbaa: Yeah. It's our motto.
Simba: What's a
C
B♭
motto? Timon: Nothin'! What's - a - motto with you?!
Pumbaa: Those two words
F
C
Slower
N.C.
Timon:
will solve all your problems.
Timon: That's right. Take Pumbaa here.
Why...
when

B♭
F
C
B♭
F
Dm7
Pumbaa:
he was a young wart - hog...
When I was a young wart -
f
ff
In tempo, brightly
C
E♭
F
Timon:
hog! Timon: Very nice.
Pumbaa: Thanks.
He found his a - ro - ma lacked a cer - tain ap - peal. He could
C
G
B♭
Pumbaa:
clear the Sa - van - nah af - ter ev - 'ry meal. I'm a sen - si - tive soul,
F
F6
C
E♭
though I seem thick - skinned. And it hurt that my
rall.

F
G
F/G
friends nev - er stood down - wind!
And oh the
tremolo
C
Timon:
shame! He was a - shamed!
Pumbaa:
Thought of chang - in' my name.
ff
3
G
Timon:
Oh, what's in a
Pumbaa:
name? And I got down - heart - ed.
B♭
Timon:
How did ya feel?
Pumbaa:
Ev - 'ry time that I...
In tempo
C
Both:
Ha - ku - na ma - ta - ta!
F
Timon: Hey, Pumbaa.
Not in front of the kids!
Pumbaa: Oh, sorry.

C
F
What a won - der - ful phrase.
Ha - ku - na ma - ta - ta!
D7
G
Am B♭dim7 G7/B
Young Simba:
E/G♯
Am
ain't no pass - ing craze.
It means no wor - ries
C/E
F
D
Young Simba, Timon & Pumbaa:
C
for the rest of your days.
It's our prob - lem - free
G7
Timon & Young Simba:
C
phi - los - o - phy.
Ha - ku - na ma - ta - ta.

C/E
F
G
C
3
C/E
F
G
Chorus:
C
Ah.
F/C
G/B
Ah.
G
F
All:
C/G
Ah.
Ha - ku - na ma - ta - ta. Ha - ku - na ma - ta - ta. Ha -
pp cresc. poco a poco

Cdim7/G
Dm/G
ku - na ma - ta - ta. Ha - ku - na ma - ta - ta. Ha - ku - na ma - ta - ta. Ha -
F/G
G
E/G#
Young Simba:
ku - na ma - ta - ta. Ha - ku - na ma - ta - ta. It means no
sfz
mf
Am
C/E
F
D7/F#
D7
All:
wor - ries for the rest of your days. It's our
C
G7
E/G#
prob - lem - free phi - los - o - phy. Ha - ku - na ma -

Am
C/E
F
G
E/G#
ta - ta.
Ha - ku - na ma - ta - ta.
Ha - ku - na ma -
f
Am
C/E
F
G
ta - ta.
Ha - ku - na ma - ta - ta.
3
C
C/E
F7
G
Pumbaa:
Timon:
Pumbaa:
Timon:
I say Ha - ku - na.
I say ma - ta - ta.
Ha - ku - na ma - ta - ta.
Ha - ku - na ma - ta - ta.
mf
C
C7/E
F
F#dim7
C/G
G
C
(Spoken:) Ta ta.
3

HE'S GOT THE WHOLE WORLD IN HIS HANDS

Traditional Spiritual

D
To Coda
whole world in His hands, He's got the
A7
D
A7
whole world in His hands.
He's got the
He's got
He's got
D
lit - tle ti - ny ba - by in His hands, He's got the
you and me, brother - er, in His hands, He's got
ev - 'ry - bod - y here in His hands, He's got
Em7
A7
Em7
A7
lit - tle ti - ny ba - by in His hands, He's got the
you and me, sis - ter, in His hands, He's got
ev - 'ry - bod - y here in His hands, He's got

D
lit - tle ti - ny ba - by in His hands, He's got the
you and me, broth - er, in His hands, He's got the
ev - 'ry - bod - y here in His hands, He's got the
A7
1,2
D
whole world in His hands. He's got the
whole world in His hands. He's got the
whole world in His
3
D
D.S. al Coda
hands. He's got the
CODA
Em7
whole world
G/A
A
D
in His hands.

HOME ON THE RANGE

Lyrics by DR. BREWSTER HIGLEY
Music by DAN KELLY

F
F7
B♭
sel - dom is heard a dis - cour - ag - ing
stood there a - mazed and asked as I
B♭m
F/C
C7
F
word, and the skies are not cloud - y all day.
gazed, if their glo - ry ex - ceeds that of ours.
Chorus
C7
F
Home, home on the range, where the
F/A
G7
Gm7
3 fr
C7
deer and the an - te - lope play; where

Additional Lyrics

3. Where the air is so pure and the zephyrs so free,
   And the breezes so balmy and light;
   Oh, I would not exchange my home on the range
   For the glittering cities so bright.
   To Chorus

4. Oh, give me a land where the bright diamond sand
   Flows leisurely down with the stream,
   Where the graceful white swan glides slowly along,
   Like a maid in a heavenly dream.
   To Chorus

THE HOKEY POKEY

Words and Music by CHARLES P. MACAK,
TAFFT BAKER and LARRY LaPRISE

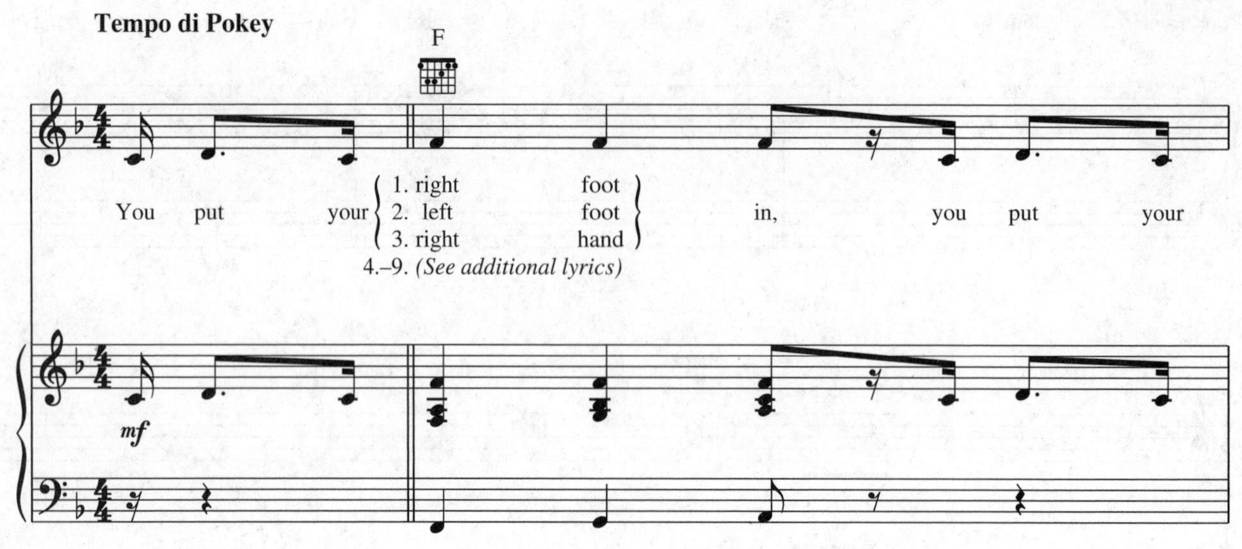

Additional Lyrics

4. Hey, you put your left hand in,
You put your left hand out.
You put your left hand in,
And you shake it all about.

5. Hey, you put your right shoulder in,
You put your right shoulder out.
You put your right shoulder in,
And you shake it all about.

6. Hey, you put your left shoulder in,
You put your left shoulder out.
You put your left shoulder in,
And you shake it all about.

7. Hey, you put your right hip in,
You put your right hip out.
You put your right hip in,
And you shake it all about.

8. Hey, you put your left hip in,
You put your left hip out.
You put your left hip in,
And you shake it all about.

9. Hey, you put your whole self in,
You put your whole self out.
You put your whole self in,
And you shake it all about.

HOT CROSS BUNS

Traditional

HUMPTY DUMPTY

Traditional

Brightly

G Am G

Hump - ty Dump - ty sat on a wall, Hump - ty

mf

Am G C G

Dump - ty had a great fall; All the King's hors - es and

C G Am G Am G

all the King's men, Could not put Hump - ty to - geth - er a - gain.

I WHISTLE A HAPPY TUNE

from THE KING AND I

Lyrics by OSCAR HAMMERSTEIN II
Music by RICHARD RODGERS

Moderato

Bb Bb/A Bb/G Bb/F Cm7

mf

F7 Bb Bb9

When - ev - er I feel a - fraid I

p

Eb Ebmaj7 Eb6 F7

hold my head e - rect And whis - tle a hap - py

F7#5 Bb N.C. F7

tune, So no one will sus - pect I'm a -

B♭(add9)
6fr
B♭
B♭maj7
B♭6
B♭
fraid. While shiv - er - ing in my
B♭9
E♭
3fr
E♭maj7
3fr
E♭6
shoes I strike a care - less pose And
F7
F7♯5
B♭
N.C.
whis - tle a hap - py tune, And no one ev - er
F7
B♭6
B♭
Cm7/B♭
6fr
B♭/D
knows I'm a - fraid. The re -
mp

G♭
G♭6
B♭
sult of this de - cep - tion is ver - y strange to
B♭6
F/C
Fm6/C
tell For when I fool the peo - ple I fear, I
C7
F7
B♭
fool my - self as well! I whis - tle a hap - py
p
B♭9
E♭
E♭maj7
E♭6
3fr
tune And ev - 'ry sin - gle time The

F7
F7♯5
B♭
N.C.
hap - pi - ness in the tune con - vinc - es me that
E♭maj7/F
F7
B♭
I'm not a - fraid.
Coda
E♭
3fr
B♭
Make be - lieve you're brave And the trick will take you far.
p
E♭
3fr
B♭
You may be as brave as you make be - lieve you

E♭
3fr
are.
Whistle
B♭
C7
You may be as
Cm7
3fr
E♭maj7/F
F7
brave
as you make be - lieve you
B♭
are.
pp
8va
p

I'M POPEYE THE SAILOR MAN

Theme from the Paramount Cartoon POPEYE THE SAILOR

Words and Music by
SAMMY LERNER

A♭
F♯dim7
E♭/G
Cm
Adim7
strong to the "fin-ich" 'cause { I eats me / he eats his } spin-ach; { I'm / he's }
B♭7
E♭
Pop - eye the Sail - or Man.
{ I'm / He's }
A♭6
B♭7
E♭
Cm
one tough Ga - zoo - kus which hates all Pa - loo - kas wot
Fm7
B♭7
E♭
ain't on the up and square.
{ I / He }

Ab6
3fr
Bb7
Eb
3fr
biffs 'em and buffs 'em an' al - ways out -
Cm
3fr
Fm7
Bb7
roughs 'em an' none of 'em gits no -
Eb
3fr
Ab
4fr
where. If an - y one
Fm7
F#dim7
Eb/G
3fr
Eb
3fr
dass - es to risk {my his} "fisk" it's

E♭7
A♭
4 fr
"Boff" an' it's "Wham," un - 'er - stan'?
C7
Fm
Fm7
B♭7
So, keep "Good Be - hav - or," that's
E♭
3 fr
Cm
3 fr
Fm
Fm7
your one life - sav - er with Pop - eye the
B♭7
E♭
3 fr
Sail - or Man.
I'm
He's

E♭
B♭7
E♭
Pop - eye the Sail - or Man,
E♭7
A♭
E♭
I'm / he's Pop - eye the Sail - or Man.
A♭
F♯dim7
E♭/G
I'm / He's strong to the "fin - ich" 'cause I eats me / he eats his
Cm
Adim7
B♭7
E♭
spin - ach; I'm / he's Pop - eye the Sail - or Man.

I'VE BEEN WORKING ON THE RAILROAD

American Folksong

Bb
A7
Bb
F
Rise up so ear - ly in the morn.
Can't you hear the cap - tain shout in',
C7
F
Bb
G7
"Di - nah, blow your horn!"
Di-nah, won't you blow,
Di - nah won't you blow,
C7
F
C
F
Di - nah won't you blow your horn?
Di - nah won't you blow
Bb
G7
C7
F
Di - nah won't you blow,
Di - nah won't you blow your horn?

C7 Gm C7

Some-one's in the kit-chen with Di - nah, Some-one's in the kit-chen I know,

F Bb F C7 F

Some-one's in the kit-chen with Di - nah, Strum-min' on the old ban - jo and sing - in',

C7 Gm C7

"Fee, fi, fid-dle-ee - i - o, Fee, fi fid-dle-ee - i - o,

F Bb F C7 F

Fee, fi, fid-dle - ee - i - o," Strum-min' on the old ban - jo.

JACK AND JILL

Traditional

I'VE GOT PEACE LIKE A RIVER

Traditional

Moderately

C7 F Dm G7 C7

mf

F B♭/F F C7 F

I've got {peace / love / joy} like a

F+ A7 B♭6 Bdim

riv - er, I've got {peace / love / joy} like a

F/C F Dm G7

riv - er, I've got {peace / love / joy} like a riv - er in my

Gm/C
3 fr
C7
F
soul.
I've got
peace
love
joy
like a
F7
B♭
C7/G
C7
riv - er,
I've got
peace
love
joy
like a
riv - er,
I've got
F
Dm
G7
C7
1,2
F
B♭/F
peace
love
joy
like a riv - er in my
soul.
F
C7
3
F
B♭/F
F
I've got
soul.

IF YOU'RE HAPPY AND YOU KNOW IT

Words and Music by
L. SMITH

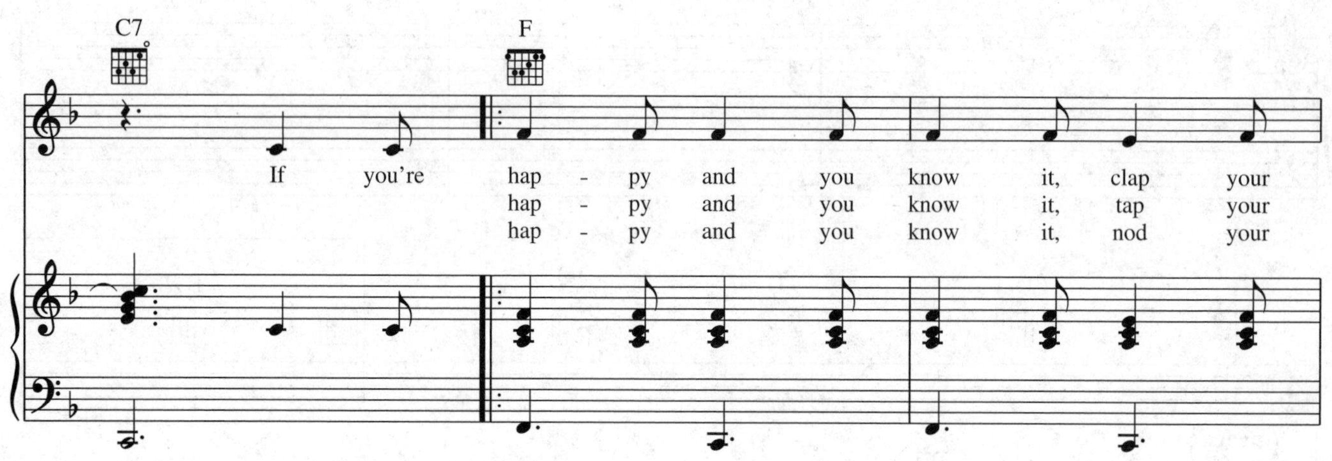

C7
F
F7
know it, clap your hands. (clap, clap) If you're
know it, tap your toe. (tap, tap) If you're
know it, nod your head. (nod, nod) If you're
B♭
F
hap - py and you know it, then your face will sure - ly
hap - py and you know it, then your face will sure - ly
hap - py and you know it, then your face will sure - ly
Gm7
C7
show it. If you're hap - py and you know it, clap your
show it. If you're hap - py and you know it, tap your
show it. If you're hap - py and you know it, nod your
1,2
F
hands. (clap, clap) If you're
toe. (tap, tap) If you're
3
F
C7
F
head. (nod, nod)

IT'S A SMALL WORLD

from "it's a small world" at Disneyland Park and Magic Kingdom Park

Words and Music by RICHARD M. SHERMAN
and ROBERT B. SHERMAN

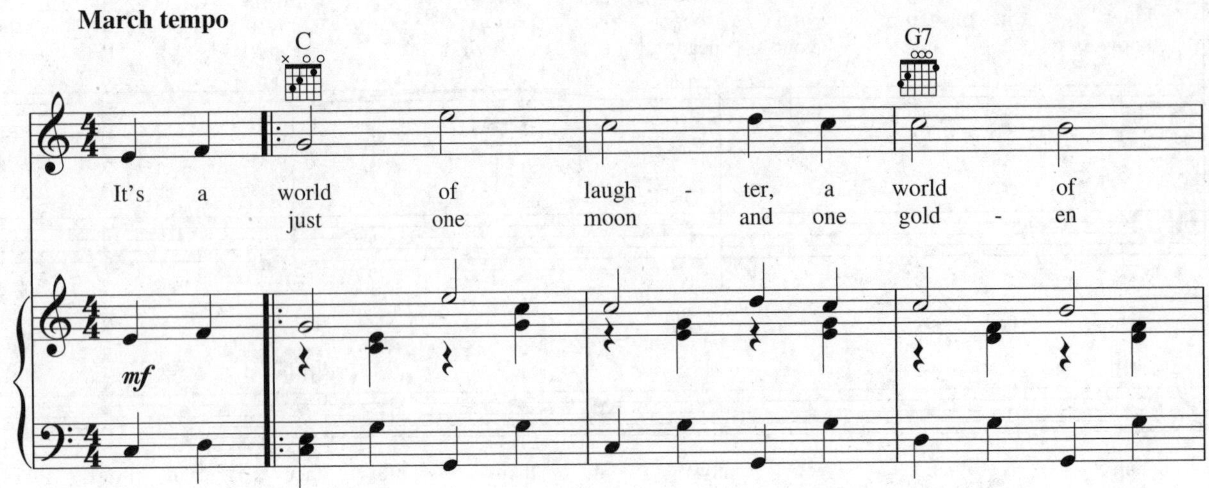

G7
C
small world af - ter all.
small world af - ter all.
It's a
G7
small world af - ter all. It's a small world
C
C7
F
Dm7
af - ter all. It's a small world af - ter all. It's a
G7
1
C
2
C
small, small world. There is world.

IT'S RAINING, IT'S POURING

Traditional

Moderate Waltz tempo

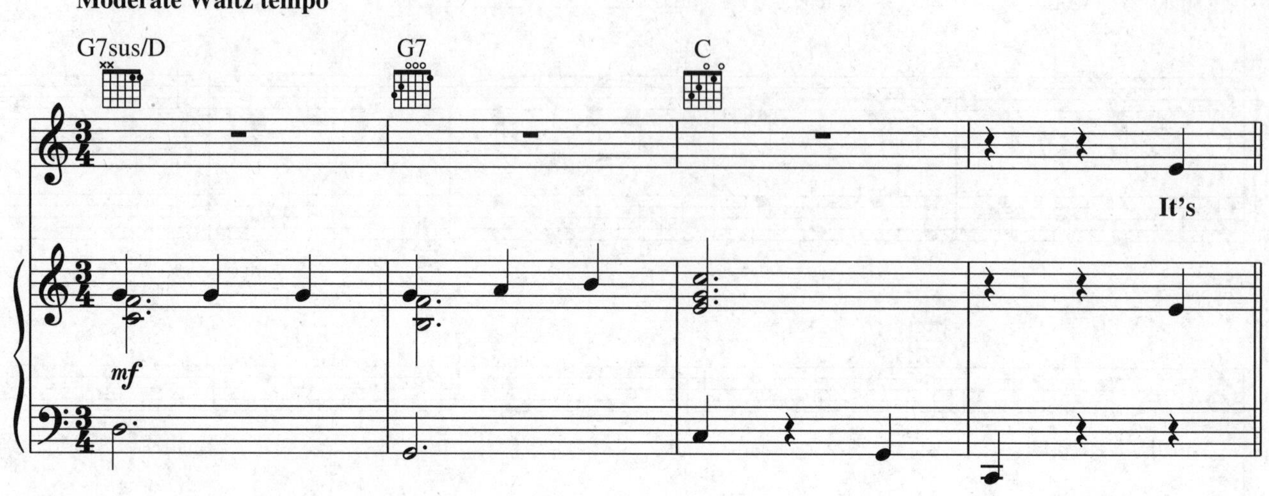

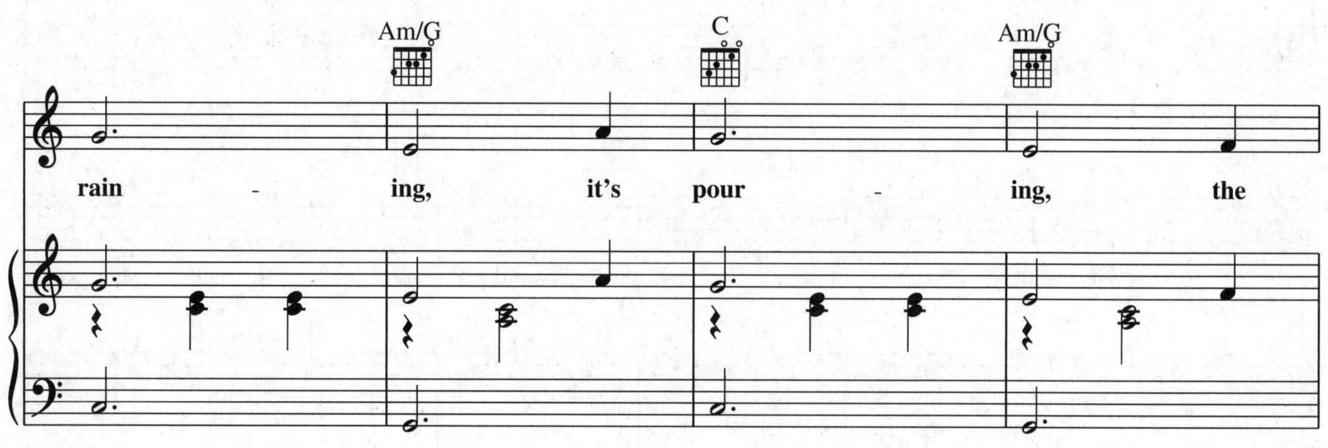

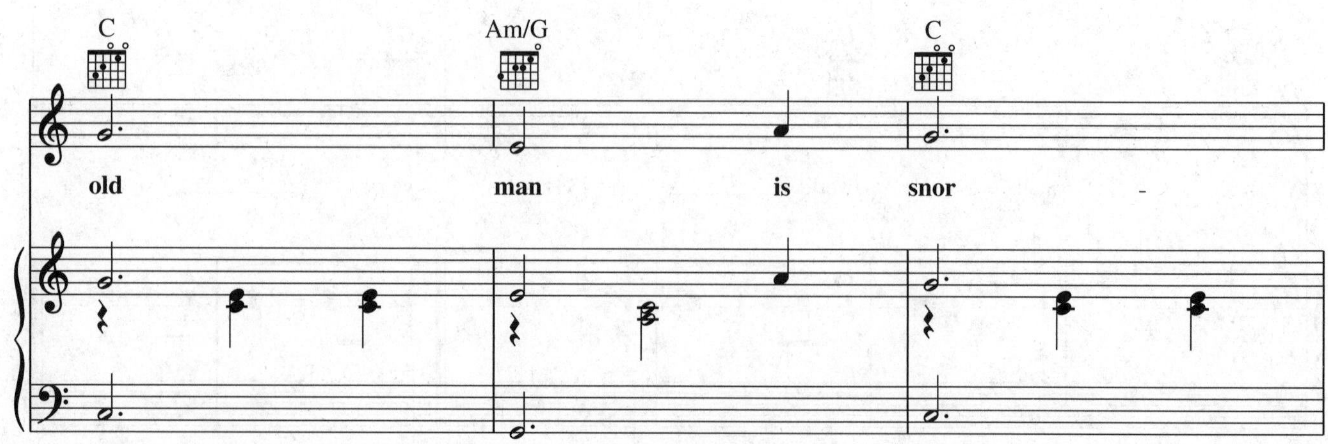

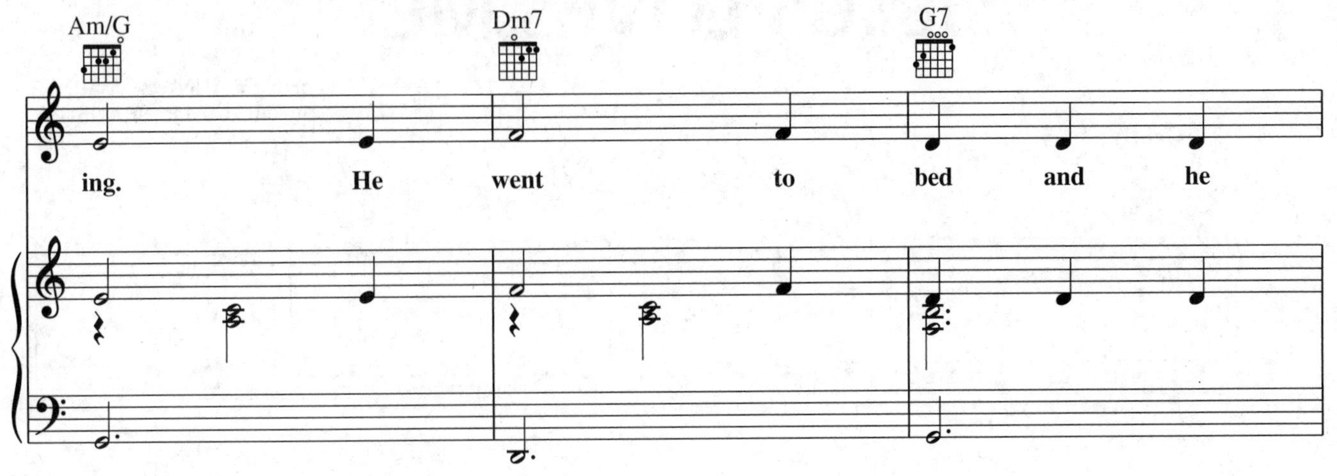
Am/G
Dm7
G7
ing. He went to bed and he

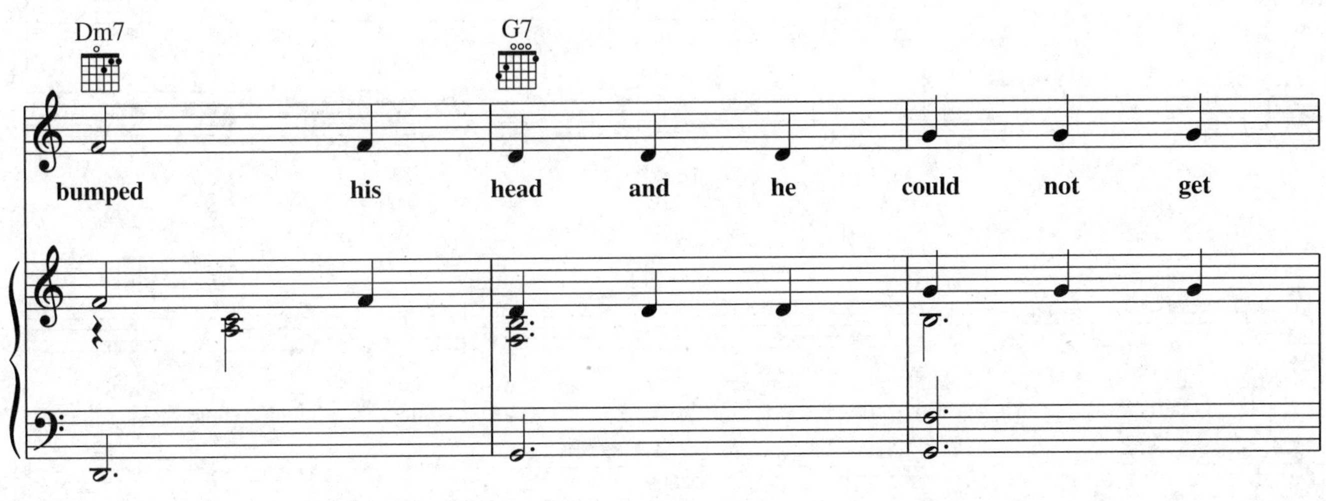
Dm7
G7
bumped his head and he could not get

C
up in the morn - ing.

JESUS LOVES ME

Words by ANNA B. WARNER
Music by WILLIAM B. BRADBURY

F
C
G7
C
G
C
loves me! The Bi - ble tells me so. Je - sus loves me! He will stay
F
C
G
C
Close be - side me all the way. He's pre - pared a home for me,
F
C
G7
C
F
C
And some - day His face I'll see. Yes, Je - sus loves me! Yes, Je - sus
G
C
F
C
G7
C
loves me! Yes, Je - sus loves me! The Bi - ble tells me so.

JIMINY CRICKET

Words by NED WASHINGTON
Music by LEIGH HARLINE

C
Dmi
C7
C
A7
D9
B7
On the hearth or in the hedge, Or may-be on your wind-ow ledge you'll
E
Cdim
C♯mi
Dmi7
G7
find me I hope you won't mind me Sing-ing
CHORUS
C
Cdim
G7
Gdim
JIM-I-NY CRICK-ET Is The Name, I'm a hap-py-go-luck-y
mf-f
G7
Cdim
G7
Gdim
G7
Gdim
G7
Gaug
C
fel-low, Al-ways get-ting in wrong For sing-ing my song, a mer-ry old soul am I.

C
Cdim
G7
Gdim
JIM - IN - Y CRICK - ET Is The Name, Got a mel - o - dy oh so
G7
Cdim
G7
Gdim
G7
Gdim
mel - low, I can bee - dle - ee - ay and bu - dle - ee - ay, And
G7
C
Gmi7
B♭m
yod - el a - way up high. I think I'm great — but
C7
F
some folks hate — The fun - ny lit - tle noise I make — To -

D7
G7
Dmi7
night I'll try a brand new break,
So sor-ry if you're kept a-wake
G7
G9
C
Cdim
yes JIM-IN-Y CRICK-ET is to blame, I'll be
G7
Gdim
G7
Cdim
G7
Gdim
hang-in' a-round this eve-ning, I'll be tip-pin' my hat, And
G7
Gdim
G7
1.
C
Gaug
2.
C
tell-in' you that: JIM-IN-Y CRICK-ET Is The Name.
Name.

JOHN JACOB JINGLEHEIMER SCHMIDT

Traditional

KUM BA YAH

Traditional Spiritual

LAVENDER BLUE

(Dilly Dilly)

from Walt Disney's SO DEAR TO MY HEART

Words by LARRY MOREY
Music by ELIOT DANIEL

Some to make hay, dilly, dilly,
Some to cut corn,
While you and I, dilly, dilly,
Keep ourselves warm.

LET THERE BE PEACE ON EARTH

Words and Music by SY MILLER
and JILL JACKSON

To Coda
B7
G7
Am
meant to be.
sol - emn vow:
With God as our
to
Em
C7
F
C/G
G7
C
Fa - ther,
broth - ers all are we.
Am7
D7
G
Let me walk with my broth - er
Am
G/D
D7
G7
D.S. al Coda
in per - fect har - mo - ny.

CODA
C
C+
take each mo - ment and live each mo - ment in
F/C
Fdim/C
Am/C
D/C
Fm6
peace e - ter - nal - ly.
C
E/G#
F/A
C/E
C7
Let there be peace on earth, and
F
Dm7
G7
Csus
3 fr
C
let it be - gin with me.

LONDON BRIDGE

Traditional

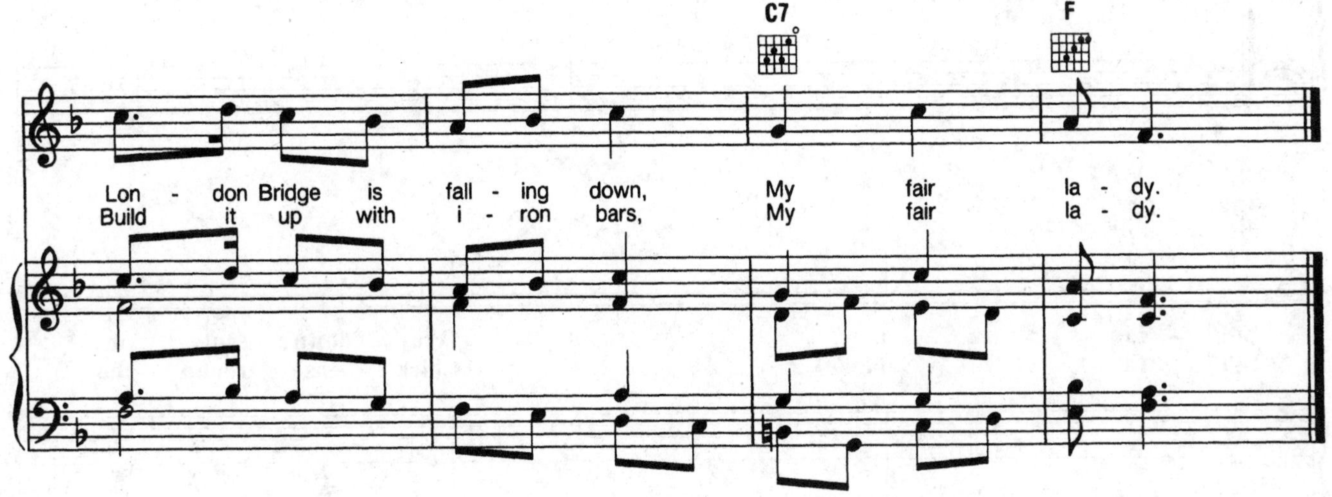

3. Iron bars will bend and break,
Bend and break, bend and break;
Iron bars will bend and break,
My fair lady.

4. Build it up with gold and silver,
Gold and silver, gold and silver;
Build it up with gold and silver,
My fair lady.

LI'L LIZA JANE
(Go Li'l Liza)

Words and Music by
COUNTESS ADA DE LACHAU

Additional Lyrics

3. I wouldn't care how far we roam, Li'l Liza Jane,
Where she's at is home sweet home, Li'l Liza Jane.
Oh, Eliza, Li'l Liza Jane!
Oh, Eliza, Li'l Liza Jane

MARY HAD A LITTLE LAMB

Words by SARAH JOSEPHA HALE
Traditional Music

G7
C
fleece was white as snow. And ev - 'ry - where that
was a - gainst the rule. It made the chil - dren
G7
C
Mar - y went, Mar - y went, Mar - y went.
laugh and play, laugh and play, laugh and play. It
Ev - 'ry - where that Mar - y went the
made the chil - dren laugh and play to
1
2
G7
C
C
lamb was sure to go. He
see a lamb at school.

MICHAEL ROW THE BOAT ASHORE

Traditional Folksong

C
F
help to trim the sail, hal - le - lu -
Riv - er is chil - ly and cold, hal - le - lu -
Riv - er is deep and wide, hal - le - lu -
C
Em
Em7
F
jah. Sis - ter, help to trim the sail, hal - le -
jah. Kills the bod - y but not the soul, hal - le -
jah. Milk and hon - ey on the oth - er side, hal - le -
1,2
3
Em/G
G7
C
C
lu - jah! Mi - chael, row
lu - jah! Mi - chael, row
lu - jah!

MICKEY MOUSE MARCH

from Walt Disney's THE MICKEY MOUSE CLUB

Words and Music by
JIMMIE DODD

F
Dm
E!
Hey, there! Hi, there! Ho, there! You're as
We play fair and we work hard and
G7
C7
F
F7
wel - come as can be!
we're in har - mo - ny!
M - I - C -
Bb
Gm7b5
F
C7
F
K - E - Y M - O - U - S - E! Mick - ey
Bb
F
Shout
Shout
Mouse Mick - ey Mouse! Mick - ey Mouse! Mick - ey Mouse! For -

Additional Interludes

5. We have fun and we play safely!
6. Look both ways when you cross crossings!
7. Don't take chances! Play with safety!
8. When you ride your bike be careful!
9. Play a little, work a little.
10. Sing a song while you are working!
11. It will make your burden lighter.
12. Do a good turn for your neighbor.
13. You can learn things while you're playing.
14. It's a lot of fun to learn things.

THE MULBERRY BUSH

Traditional

4. This is the way we scrub the floor, *etc.*
So early Wednesday morning.

5. This is the way we mend our clothes, *etc.*
So early Thursday morning.

6. This is the way we sweep the house, *etc.*
So early Friday morning.

7. This is the way we bake our bread, *etc.*
So early Saturday morning.

8. This is the way we go to church, *etc.*
So early Sunday morning.

THE MUFFIN MAN

Traditional

B♭6
C7
F
Gm7
3 fr
lives in Dru - ry Lane? Yes, we know the
F/A
B♭
G7/B
muf - fin man, the muf - fin man, the
C7
F
Gm7
3 fr
muf - fin man. Yes, we know the
F/A
B♭6
C7
F
muf - fin man who lives in Dru - ry Lane.
sfz

THE MUPPET SHOW THEME

from the Television Series

Words and Music by JIM HENSON
and SAM POTTLE

C
E♭dim7
G7
C
E♭dim7
G7
It's time to put on make - up. It's time to dress up right.
C
C/B♭
F/A
Fm/A♭
G13
C
It's time to raise the cur - tain on The Mup - pet Show to - night. To
F
Fm
C
F
E7
Am
Am/G
in - tro - duce this rec - ord, that's what I'm here to do. So it
F
E7
A7sus
A7
D7sus
D7
G7
real - ly makes me hap - py to in - tro - duce to you
Spoken: the first, original, genuine, no money back guarantee Muppet Show Cast Album!

C Ebdim7 G7 C Ebdim7 G7
Sung: It's time to put on make - up. It's time to dress up right.
C C/Bb F/A Fm/Ab C/G F#m7b5
It's time to get things start - ed on the most sen - sa - tion - al, in - spi - ra - tion - al,
cresc. poco a poco
Fmaj7 F/E Dm7
cel - e - bra - tion - al, mup - pet - a - tion - al... This is what we call The
G13b9 3fr C
Mup - pet Show!
ff
8va
8vb.

MY BONNIE LIES OVER THE OCEAN

Traditional

G C G

Bon - nie lies o - ver the o - cean,

A7 D7

oh, bring back my Bon - nie to

G D7 G

me. Bring

G/B C A7/C#

back, bring back, oh,

D7
G
D7
bring back my Bon - nie to me, to
G
G/B
me. Bring back,
C
A7/C♯
D7
bring back, oh, bring back my
G
Bon - nie to me.
p

MY FAVORITE THINGS

from THE SOUND OF MUSIC

Lyrics by OSCAR HAMMERSTEIN II
Music by RICHARD RODGERS

Em
Cream col - ored pon - ies and crisp ap - ple
mf
mp
Cmaj7
strud - els, Door - bells and sleigh - bells and schnitz - el with noo - dles,
Am7
D7
G/B
C/E
G/D
Wild geese that fly with the moon on their wings, These are a
C
F♯m7♭5
4fr
B7
E
few of my fa - vor - ite things.
f

A
Girls in white dress - es with blue sat - in sash - es, Snow - flakes that
mf
Am7
D7
stay on my nose and eye - lash - es, Sil - ver white win - ters that
G/B
C/E
G/D
C
F♯m7♭5
4fr
B7
melt in - to springs, These are a few of my fa - vor - ite things.
Em
F♯m7♭5
4fr
B7
When the dog bites, When the bee stings,
mf

Em
C
When I'm feel - ing sad,
I
A7/C♯
A7
sim - ply re - mem - ber my fa - vor - ite things and
G/D
C/D
G/D
C/D
G
D7♭9
4fr
D7
G
then I don't feel so bad.
cresc.
f
C
G/D
D7
G
sf

THE NAME GAME

By LINCOLN CHASE
and SHIRLEY ELLISTON

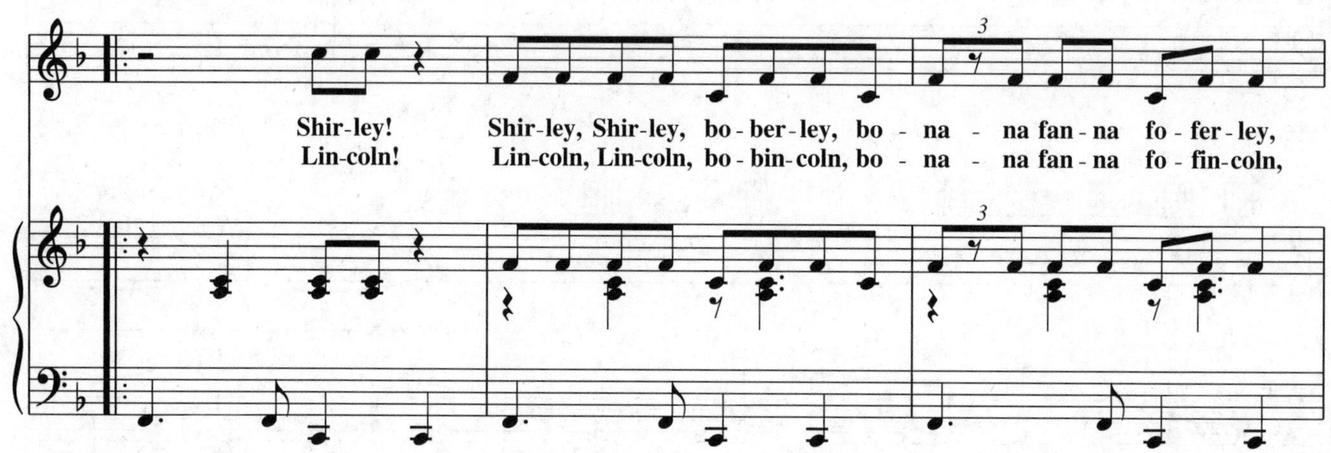

F7
F
F7
F
Come on ev - 'ry - bod - y.
I say now
F7
F
F7
F
B♭7
let's play a game.
I bet - cha I can make a rhyme
F7
F
F7
F
out of an - y - bod - y's name.
The first
F7
F
F7
F
let - ter of the name,
I treat it like it was - n't there.

F7
F
B♭7
But a "B" or an "F," or an
F7
F
"M" will ap - pear.
And then I say
"Bo"
"Bo"
add a "B"
then
now
I
say the name, then "Bo - na - na, fan - na" and
To - ny with a "B," now "Bo - na - na, fan - na" and
F7
B♭7
"fo." And then I say the name a - gain with an
"fo." And now you say the name a - gain with an

F7
"f" ver - y plain, then a "fee fi" and a "mo." And then I
"f" ver - y plain, then "fee fi" and a "mo." And then you
B♭7
F7
say the name a - gain with an "M" this time. And there is - n't an - y name that
say the name a - gain with an "M" this time. And there is - n't an - y name that
F
To Coda
I can't rhyme.
you can't rhyme.
Ar - nold!
To - ny!
F
3
Ar - nold, Ar - nold, bo - bar - nold, bo - na - na, fan - na fo - far - nold,

B♭7
F
fee fi mo-mar-nold. Ar-nold!
B♭7
But if the first two let-ters are ev-er the same,
F
drop them both, then say the name. Like Bob, Bob, drop the
"B's." Bo - ob, or Fred. Fred, drop the "F's." Fo - red, or

B♭7
F
Mar - y, Mar - y, drop the "M's," Mo - ar - y.
That's the on - ly rule that
is con - tra - ry.
D.S. al Coda
Say
CODA
F
3
To - ny, To - ny, bo - bo - ney, bo - na - na fan - na, fo - fo - ney,
Bil - ly, Bil - ly, bo - il - ly, bo - na - na fan - na, fo - fil - ly,
Mar - sha, Mar - sha, bo - bar - sha, bo - na - na fan - na, fo - far - sha,
3
B♭7
F
fee fi mo - mo - ney. To - ny!
fee fi mo - mil - ly. Bil - ly!
fee fi mo - ar - sha. Mar - sha!

1, 2
3
Let's do Bil - ly! Lit - tle trick with Nick!
Let's do Mar - sha!
Nick, Nick, bo - bick, bo - na - na fan - na, fo - fick,
B♭7
F
fee fi mo - mick. Nick! The
name game.

OH WHERE, OH WHERE HAS MY LITTLE DOG GONE

Words by SEP. WINNER
Traditional Melody

OH! SUSANNA

Words and Music by
STEPHEN C. FOSTER

C7
F
night I left, The weath - er was so dry, The sun so hot I
C7
F
froze my - self, Su - san - na, don't you cry.
B♭
Gm
C7
F
B♭
G7
C7
Oh, Su - san - na! Oh, don't you cry for me, For I
F
C7
F
come from Al - a - bam - a with my ban - jo on my knee.

THE OLD GRAY MARE

Words and Music by
J. WARNER

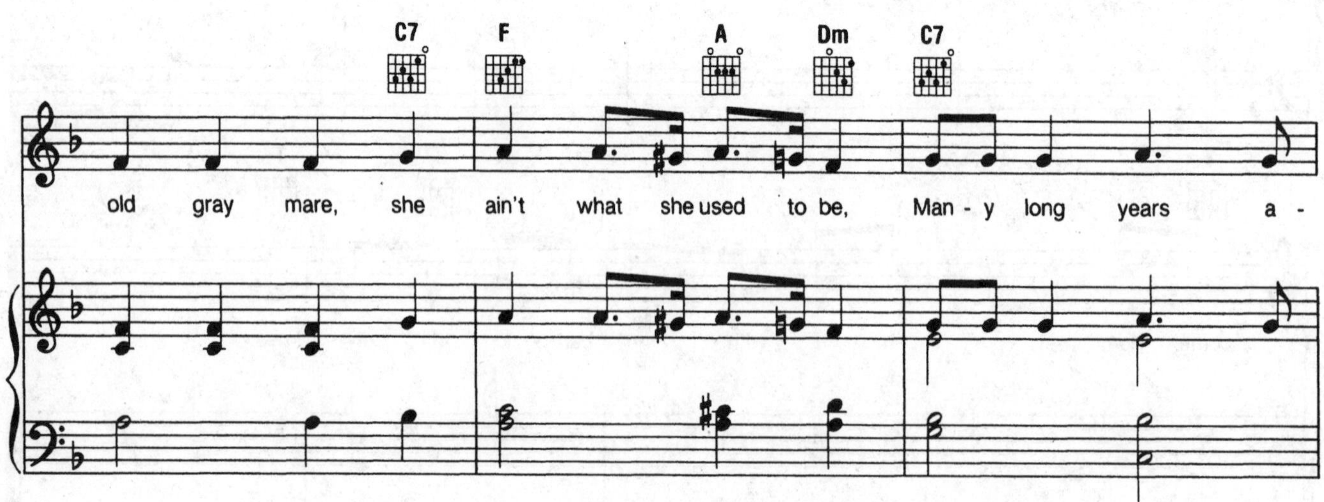

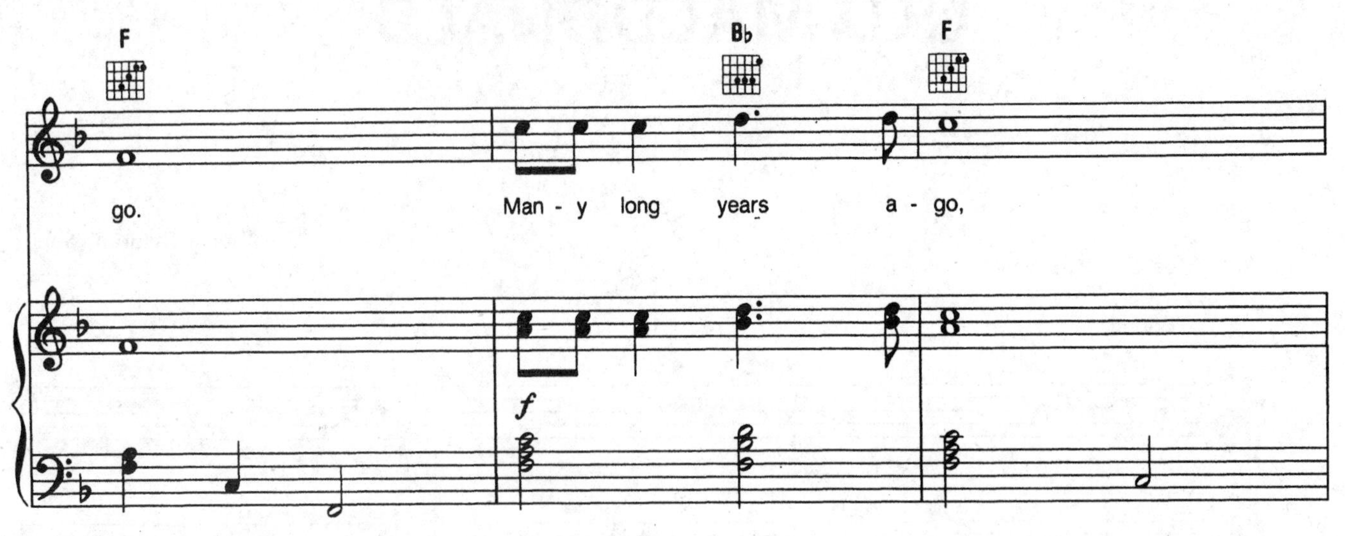
F
B♭
F
go.
Man - y long years a - go,
f

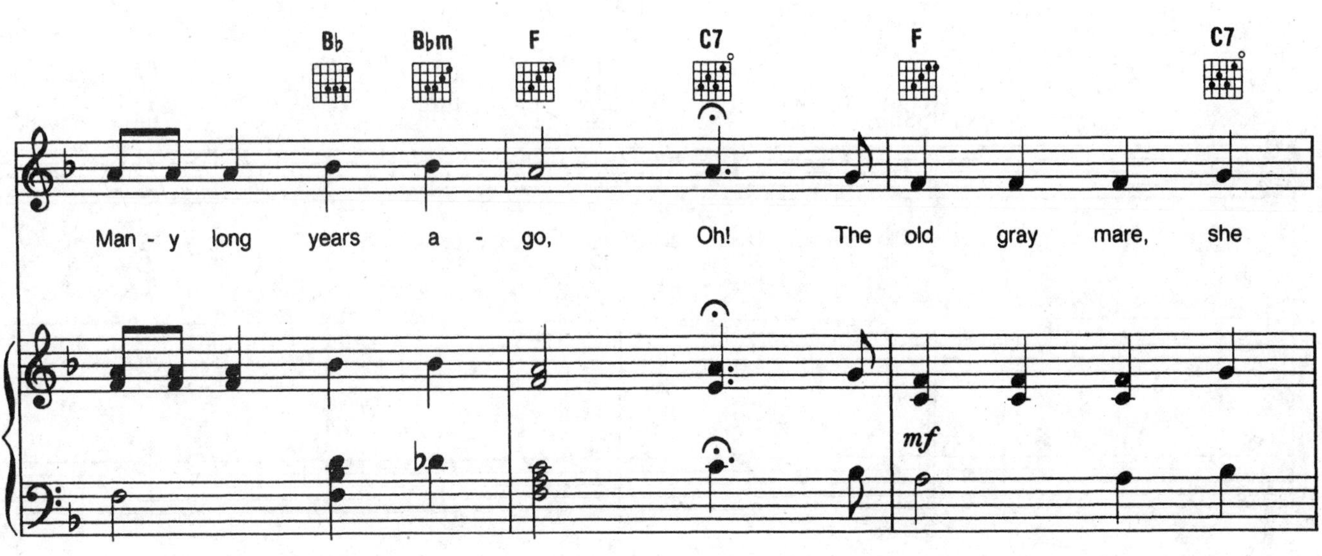
B♭
B♭m
F
C7
F
C7
Man - y long years a - go,
Oh! The old gray mare, she
mf

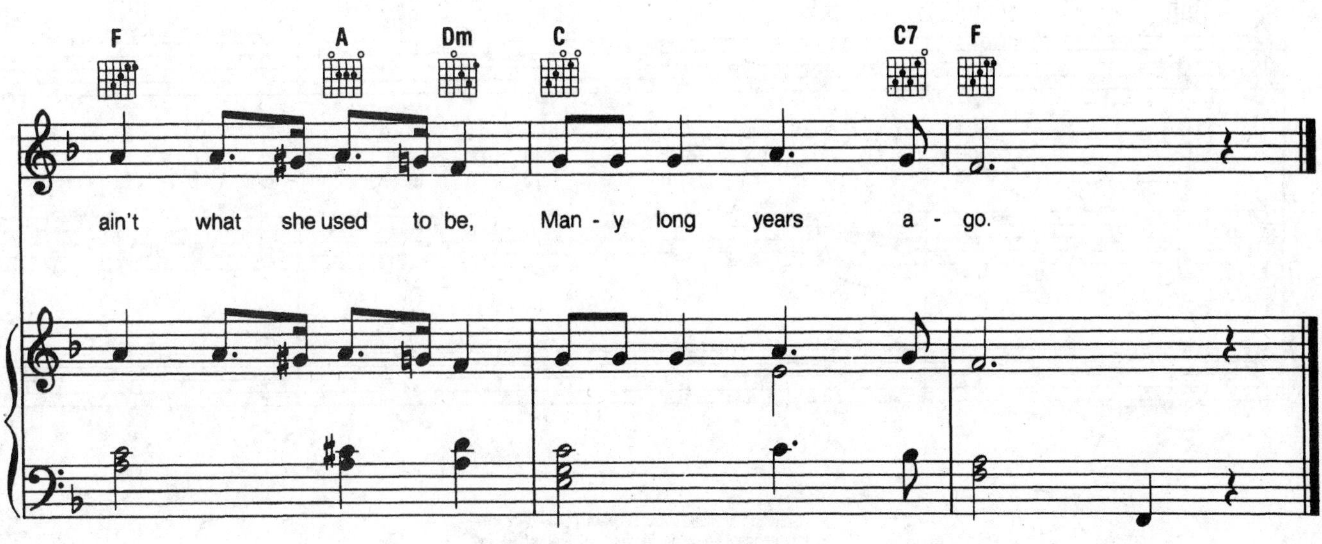
F
A
Dm
C
C7
F
ain't what she used to be, Man - y long years a - go.

OLD MACDONALD

Traditional Children's Song

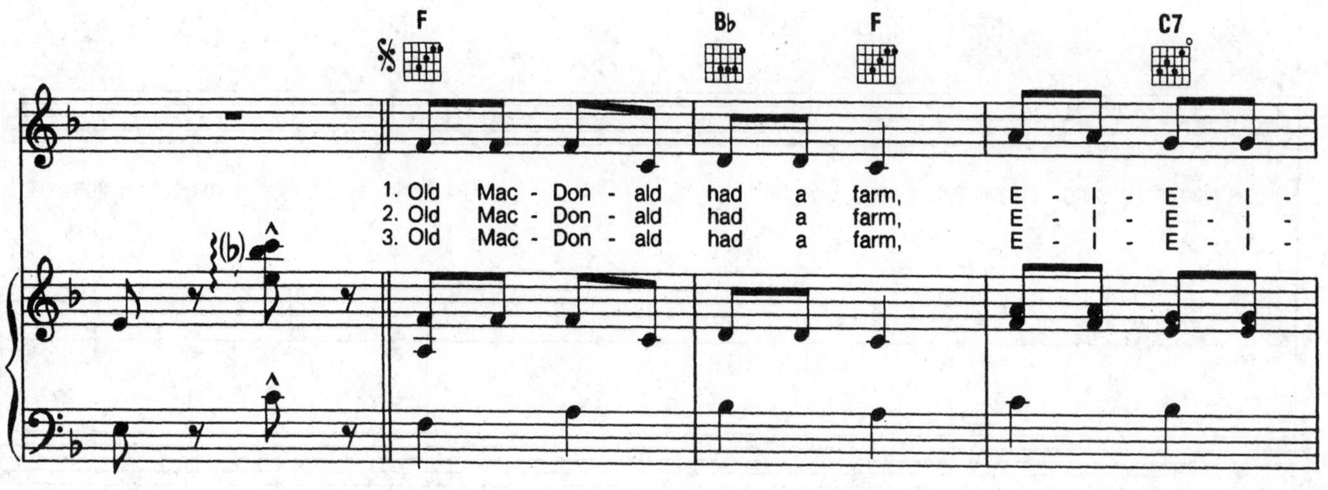

4. Old MacDonald had a farm,
   E-I-E-I-O,
   And on his farm he had a horse,
   E-I-E-I-O,
   With a neigh-neigh here and a neigh-neigh there, *etc.*

5. Old MacDonald had a farm,
   E-I-E-I-O,
   And on his farm he had a donkey,
   E-I-E-I-O,
   With a hee-haw here, *etc.*

6. Old MacDonald had a farm,
   E-I-E-I-O,
   And on his farm he had some chickens,
   E-I-E-I-O,
   With a chick-chick here, *etc.*

For additional verses, add your own animals.

ON THE GOOD SHIP LOLLIPOP

from BRIGHT EYES

Words and Music by SIDNEY CLARE
and RICHARD A. WHITING

G7
ev - 'ry - where, crack - er - jack bands fill the air, And
C
there you are hap - py land - ing on a choc - o - late bar,
Bb/C
C7
F
Adim
C7
C7+5
See the sug - ar bowl do a toot - sie roll with the
F
C+
F
Fmaj7
Am7
D7
big bad dev - il's food cake. If you eat too much

Am9
D7
G
Adim/G
3fr
Fm6/G
G7
ooh! ooh! You'll a - wake with a "tum - my" ache, On the
C
G7
Good Ship Lol - li - pop, it's a night trip in - to
bed you hop with this com - mand: "All a - board for
and dream a - way On the Good Ship
1 C
2 C
C6/9
can - dy land." On the Lol - li - pop!
mf

PETER COTTONTAIL

Words and Music by STEVE NELSON
and JACK ROLLINS

C Cmaj7 C7 F Fmaj7 F6 F
Bring - in' ev - 'ry girl and boy bas - kets full of Eas - ter joy,
"Try to do the things you should." May - be if you're ex - tra good,
He's the king of Bun - ny Land, 'cause his eyes are shin - y and
Some - thing told him it was wrong, Farm - er Jones might come a - long
G7 C♯dim7 G7 C F
things to make your Eas - ter bright and gay.
he'll roll lots of Eas - ter eggs your way.
he can spot the wolf a mile a - way.
and an aw - ful price he'd have to pay.
C C7 F F+ F6
He's got jel - ly beans for Tom - my, col - ored
You'll wake up on Eas - ter morn - ing and you'll
When the oth - ers go for clo - ver and the
But he knew his legs were fast - er so he
C C7 F F+
eggs for sis - ter Sue, there's an or - chid for your
know that he was there when you find those choc -
big bad wolf ap - pears, he's the one that's watch - ing
nib - bled three or four, and he al - most met dis -

F6 Am D7 G G7♯5
Mom - my and an Eas - ter bon - net, too. Oh!
bun - nies that he's hid - ing ev - 'ry - where. Oh!
o - ver giv - in' sig - nals with his ears. And
as - ter when he heard that shot - gun roar. Oh,
C Cmaj7 C7 F Fmaj7
Here comes Pe - ter Cot - ton - tail, hop - pin' down the
Here comes Pe - ter Cot - ton - tail, hop - pin' down the
that's why folks in Rab - bit town feel so free when
that's how Pe - ter Cot - ton - tail hop - pin down the
mf
F6 F G7/D C♯dim7 G7/D G7
bun - ny trail; hip - pi - ty hop - pi - ty, Hap - py Eas - ter
bun - ny trail; hip - pi - ty hop - pi - ty, Hap - py Eas - ter
he's a - roun' Pe - ter's help - in' some - one ev - 'ry
bun - ny trail; lost his tail, but still he got a -
1 C C♯dim7 Dm7 G7
day.
day.
2 C F C
day.
way.

ON TOP OF SPAGHETTI

Words and Music by
TOM GLAZER

F
C
N.C.
F
It rolled off the ta - ble and
The mush was as tast - y as
So if you eat spa - ghet - ti all
C
G7
on - to the floor, and then my poor meat - ball
tast - y could be, and ear - ly next sum - mer,
cov - ered with cheese, hold on to your meat - balls
1, 2
C
F
rolled out of the door.
it grew in - to a tree.
and don't ev - er
C
N.C.
3
C
F
C
It rolled in the sneeze. A - choo!
The tree was all

POLLY WOLLY DOODLE

Traditional American Minstrel Song

4. Oh, I went to bed, but it wasn't no use,
Singing polly-wolly-doodle all the day.
My feet stuck out like a chicken roost,
Singing polly-wolly-doodle all the day.
Chorus

5. Behind the barn down on my knees,
Singing polly-wolly-doodle all the day.
I thought I heard a chicken sneeze,
Singing polly-wolly-doodle all the day.
Chorus

6. He sneezed so hard with the whooping cough,
Singing polly-wolly-doodle all the day.
He sneezed his head and tail right off,
Singing polly-wolly-doodle all the day.
Chorus

POP GOES THE WEASEL

Traditional

A7
Bm
F♯m
spool___ of thread, A pen - ny for a nee - dle,
G
Em
Bm
G
A7
D
That's the way the mon - ey goes, Pop! Goes the wea - sel.
2
Fdim7
A7
Bm
F♯m
got no time to wait___ and sigh, no patience to wait 'til by and by, So
G
Em
Bm
G
A7
D
kiss me quick I'm off good - bye Pop! Goes the wea - sel.

PUFF THE MAGIC DRAGON

Words by LENNY LIPTON
Music by PETER YARROW

B7
E
A
land called Hon - a - lee.
Lit - tle Jack - ie
C♯m
4fr
D
A
Pa - per loved that ras - cal Puff and
D
A
F♯m
B7
E
brought him strings and seal - ing wax and oth - er fan - cy
A
E
A
C♯m
4fr
Chorus
stuff. Oh! Puff the Mag - ic Drag - on

D
A
D
lived by the sea and frol - icked in the
A
F♯m
B7
E
au - tumn mist in a land called Hon - a - lee.
A
C♯m
4fr
D
Puff the Mag - ic Drag - on lived by the
A
D
A
F♯m
sea and frol - icked in the au - tumn mist in a

Additional Lyrics

2. Together they would travel on a boat with billowed sail.
   Jackie kept a lookout perched on Puff's gigantic tail.
   Noble kings and princes would bow whene'er they came.
   Pirate ships would low'r their flag when Puff roared out his name. Oh! *(To Chorus)*

3. A dragon lives forever, but not so little boys.
   Painted wings and giant rings make way for other toys.
   One gray night it happened, Jackie Paper came no more,
   And Puff that mighty dragon, he ceased his fearless roar.

4. His head was bent in sorrow, green tears fell like rain.
   Puff no longer went to play along the Cherry Lane.
   Without his lifelong friend, Puff could not be brave,
   So Puff that mighty dragon sadly slipped into his cave. Oh! *(To Chorus)*

* THE RETURN OF PUFF

5. Puff the Magic Dragon danced down the Cherry Lane.
   He came upon a little girl, Julie Maple was her name.
   She'd heard that Puff had gone away, but that can never be,
   So together they went sailing to the land called Honalee. *(To Chorus)*

THE RAINBOW CONNECTION

from THE MUPPET MOVIE

Words and Music by PAUL WILLIAMS
and KENNETH L. ASCHER

A E/G♯ F♯m7 A/E D(add2) D(add2)/A
rain - bows have noth - ing to hide.
look what it's done so far.
Dmaj7
So we've been told, and some choose to be - lieve it.
What's so a - maz - ing that keeps us star - gaz - ing, and
G♯m/C♯
4fr
I know they're wrong; wait and see.
what do we think we might see?
Bm7 E D/E C♯m7 E/F♯ F♯7
2fr
4fr
Some - day we'll find it, the Rain - bow Con - nec - tion; the
Some - day we'll find it, the Rain - bow Con - nec - tion; the

Bm7
2fr
E7sus
E7
1
A
D/A
lov - ers, the dream - ers, and me.
lov - ers, the dream - ers, and
A
D/A
2
A
E/G#
me. All of us
F#m7
A/E
D(add2)
A/C#
un - der its spell; we know that it's prob - a - bly
D6/E
Eb6/F
F(add2)
F
Bb(add2)
mag - ic. Have you been

F/G
Gm7
Cm7
Eb/F
F
Bb
F/A
half a - sleep and have you heard voic - es? I've heard them
Gm7
Bb/F
Eb(add2)
Eb/F
Fsus
Bb
F/G
Gm7
call - ing my name. Is this the sweet sound that
Cm7
Eb/F
F
Bb
F/A
Gm7
Eb(add2)
calls the young sail - ors? The voice might be one and the same.
Eb
Ebmaj7
I've heard it too man - y times to ig -

Am/D
nore it. It's some - thing that I'm s'posed to be.
Cm7
F
E♭/F
Dm7
F/G
G7
Some - day we'll find it, the Rain - bow Con - nec - tion; the
Cm7
F7sus
F7
B♭
F/A
Gm7
lov - ers the dream-ers, and me. La da da dee da da
B♭/F
E♭(add2)
E♭
Fsus
F7
B♭
do la la da da da de da do.
L.H.

RUBBER DUCKIE

from the Television Series SESAME STREET

Words and Music by
JEFF MOSS

B♭ B♭7+5 E♭ E♭m6 B♭/D Gm7
When I squeeze you, you make noise. Rub - ber Duck - ie, you're my
Cm7 F7 B♭ Em7-5 A7 Dm
ver - y best friend it's true. Oh, ev - 'ry day when I
A7 Dm B♭m F/C
make my way to the tub - by I find a lit - tle fel - low who's
Gm7/C Cm7 F7 B♭ Bdim
cute and yel - low and chub - by, rub - a - dub - dub - by, Rub - ber Duck - ie,

Cm7 F7 B♭ B♭7+5 E♭ E♭m6
you're so fine, and I'm luck - y that you're mine.
1 B♭/D Gm7 Cm7 F7 B♭ Bdim Cm7 F7
Rub - ber Duck - ie, I'm aw - ful - ly fond of you.
2 B♭/D Gm7 Cm7 F7 B♭/D Gm7
Rub - ber Duck - ie, I'd like a whole pond of Rub - ber Duck - ie, I'm
Cm7 F7 B♭ Gm7 C7-9 F7-9 B♭
aw - ful - ly fond of you.

ROCK-A-MY SOUL

African-American Spiritual

C/D
D
Bm
F♯m
G/A
A7
val - ley to pray, oh, rock - a - my soul, my soul got hap - py and I
val - ley at night, oh, rock - a - my soul, I knew that ev - 'ry-thing would
morn-ing be - fore, oh, rock - a - my soul, I found the peace that I was
cloud - i - est day, oh, rock - a - my soul, a prayer is all you need to
1-3
4
D.S. al Coda
stayed all day,
be al - right,
look - ing for,
light your way,
oh, rock - a - my soul. Oh, soul. Oh,
CODA
Oh, rock - a - my soul!
E
G
A

ROW, ROW, ROW YOUR BOAT

Traditional

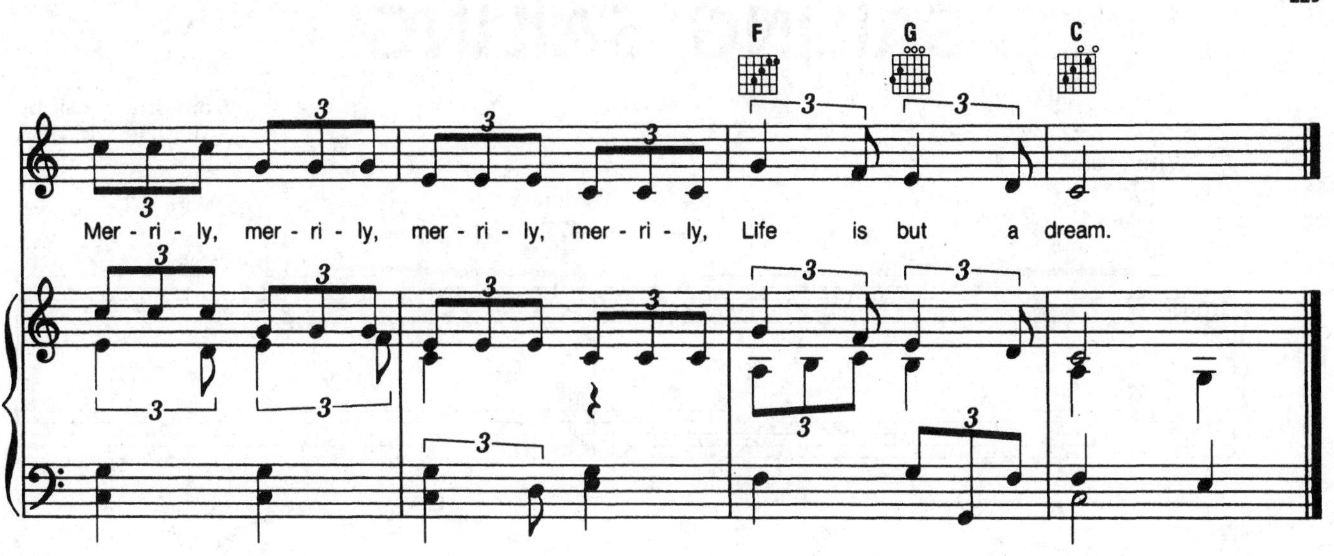

A SUGGESTED ACTIVITY

"Row, Row, Row Your Boat" is a famous "round" that has been sung and enjoyed by people of all ages. When sung correctly, the melody actually goes around and around. Here's how it works: The singers are divided into two groups. The first group sings the first line alone. At this point, the second group starts at the beginning, while the first group continues with the second line. In this manner, the groups are always exactly one line apart as the tune is repeated. The last time through, the second group sings the final line alone just as the first group sang the opening line alone. Try it. . . it's fun!

SAILING, SAILING

Words and Music by
GODFREY MARKS

D7
G7
C
Jack comes home a - gain.
Sail - ing,
F
sail - ing, o - ver the bound - ing
C
F
E
main.
For man - y a storm - y
mf
cresc.
Am
Fm6/A♭
6fr
C/G
G7
C
wind shall blow, ere Jack comes home a - gain.
f

SESAME STREET THEME

Words by BRUCE HART,
JON STONE and JOE RAPOSO
Music by JOE RAPOSO

B♭
F
C7
Dm7/C
C7
Dm7/C
how to get to Ses - a - me Street?
C
Dm7/C
C7
Dm7/C
A
It's a mag - ic car -
Bm7/A
E7/A
A
Bm7/A
E7
- pet ride.
Ev - 'ry door will o - pen wide to hap - py
A
E9/A
A
D9/A
D/A
A
peo - ple like you.
Hap - py peo - ple like...
What a beau - ti - ful

C
F7
C
sun - ny day sweep - in' the clouds a -
F7
C
F7
G7/D
Dm7
G7/D
way. On my way to where the air is sweet.
G7
F9
G7/D
B♭
F
C
Dm7/C
Can you tell me how to get, how to get to Ses - a-me Street?
C7
Dm7/C
C
Dm7/C
C7
Dm7/C
C7
How to get to Ses - a-me Street?

SING

from SESAME STREET

Words and Music by
JOE RAPOSO

Gm7
C9
Cm7
F7
Sing of hap - py, not sad.
B♭
Cm7
Sing! Sing a song. Make it
B♭
B♭maj7
3fr
B♭6
Fm7/B♭
B♭7
Fm7/B♭
B♭7
sim - ple to last your whole life long. Don't
E♭maj7
D7
Gm7
C9
wor - ry that it's not good e - nough for an - y - one else to hear.

Cm7
F7
Bb
F7
Sing! Sing a song!
Bb
Bbmaj7
3fr
Ebmaj7
La la do la da, La da la do la da, La da da la do la da.
Bb
Bbmaj7
3fr
Ebmaj7
1.
La do la da, La da la la da, Lo da da la do lo da.
Repeat and fade
Bb
Bbmaj7
3fr
Ebmaj7
2.
La la do la da, La da la do la da, La da da la do la da.
Repeat and fade

SHE'LL BE COMIN' 'ROUND THE MOUNTAIN

Traditional

3. Oh, we'll all go to meet her when she comes,
Oh, we'll all go to meet her when she comes,
Oh, we'll all go to meet her,
Oh, we'll all go to meet her,
Oh, we'll all go to meet her when she comes.

4. We'll be singin' "Hallelujah" when she comes,
We'll be singin' "Hallelujah" when she comes,
We'll be singin' "Hallelujah,"
We'll be singin' "Hallelujah,"
We'll be singin' "Hallelujah" when she comes.

SKIP TO MY LOU

Traditional

Gaily

F C7

Ti Ti-ka Ta

Lou, Lou, Skip to my Lou, Lou, Lou, Skip to my Lou,

mf

F C7 F

Lou, Lou, Skip to my Lou, Skip to my Lou, my dar - ling.

C7

1. Lost my part - ner, what'll I do? Lost my part - ner, what'll I do?
2, 3, 4, 5, 6

2. I'll find another one, prettier than you,
   I'll find another one, prettier than you,
   I'll find another one, prettier than you,
   Skip to my Lou, my darling.

3. Little red wagon, painted blue.

4. Can't get a red bird, a blue bird'll do.

5. Cows in the meadow, moo, moo, moo.

6. Flies in the buttermilk, shoo, shoo, shoo.

SO LONG, FAREWELL

from THE SOUND OF MUSIC

C
Dm
G7
C
BRIGITTA, GRETL, MARTA:
"coo - coo"
"coo - coo"
"coo - coo"
"coo - coo"
coo."
Re - gret-ful - ly they tell us, But firm-ly they com-pel us To
Allegro
Dm7
G9
C
"coo - coo" to you.
say good - bye to you.
mf
R.H.
ALL CHILDREN:
MARTA:
So long, fare - well, Auf wie - der - sehn, good - night, I

G7
hate to go and miss this pret - ty sight. —
mf
C
R.H.
CHILDREN:
So long, fare - well, Auf wie - der - sehn, a - dieu, —
KURT:
a - dieu, A - dieu, to yieu and yieu and yieu. —
G7
mf

C
R.H.
CHILDREN:
So long, fare - well, Au' - voir, Auf wie - der - sehn,
LIESL:
I'd
like to stay and taste my first cham - pagne.
G7
mf
C
R.H.

CHILDREN:
So long, fare - well, Auf wie - der - sehn, good - bye,
FRIEDRICH:
I leave and heave a sigh and say good - bye, good - bye.
G7
Cmaj7
Meno mosso
BRIGITTA:
I'm glad to go, I can - not tell a lie.
LOUISA:
I flit, I float, I
p
p legato

G7
fleet - ly flee, I fly.
Molto tranquillo
C6
G9/C
GRETL:
C6
G9/C
C6
G9/C
ALL CHILDREN:
The sun has gone to bed and so must I. So
f
pp
F/A
C/G
F
C/E
D7
long, fare - well, Auf wie - der - sehn, good - bye, Good - bye; Good -
mf
dolce
G9
Cadd9
pp
GUESTS:
bye, Good - bye, Good - bye!
8va
rall.

SPLISH SPLASH

Words and Music by BOBBY DARIN
and MURRAY KAUFMAN

C7
F7
Cm7
Think - in' ev - 'ry - thing was all right. Well, I
teens had the danc - in' bug. There was
Bb
stepped out the tub put my feet on the floor, I
Lol - li - pop with Peg - gy Sue. Good
Eb
Edim7
F
F7
wrapped the towel a - round me and I o - pened the door. And then - a
gol - ly, Miss Mol - ly was - a e - ven there too. A well - a
Bb
F7
Splish splash, I jumped back in the bath, Well,
Splish splash, I for - got a - bout the bath, I

Bb
1
how was I to know there was a par - ty go - ing on?
went and put my danc - ing shoes—
2
Bb
on I was a - splish - in' and a - splash - in', I was a -
roll - in' and a - stroll - in', I was a - mov - in' and a - groov - in',
Eb7
Bb
Repeat and Fade
I was a - reel - in' with the feel - in' I was a -

A SPOONFUL OF SUGAR

from Walt Disney's MARY POPPINS

Words and Music by RICHARD M. SHERMAN
and ROBERT B. SHERMAN

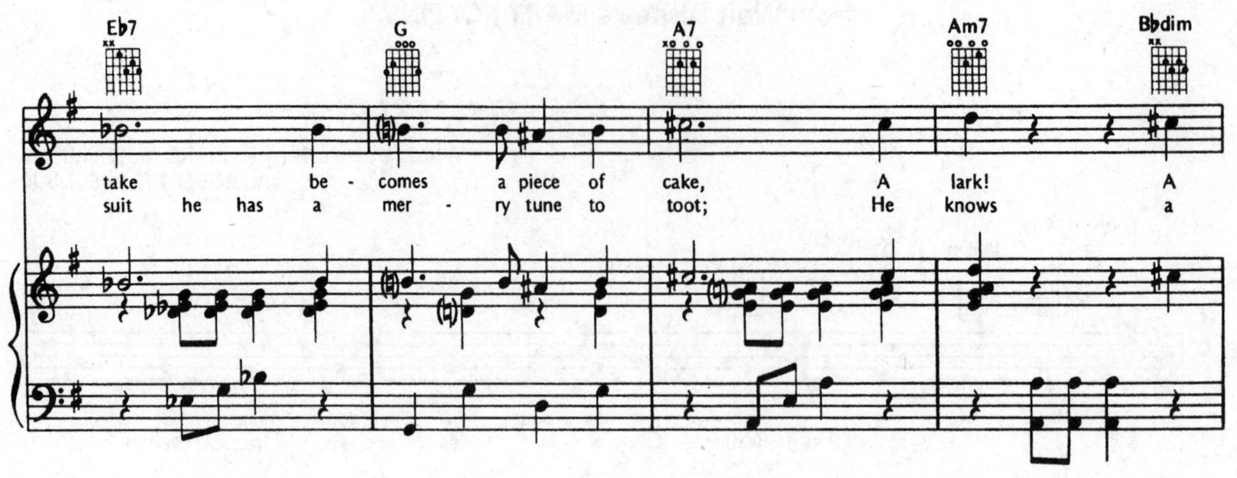
Eb7
G
A7
Am7
Bbdim
take be - comes a piece of cake, A lark! A
suit he has a mer - ry tune to toot; He knows a

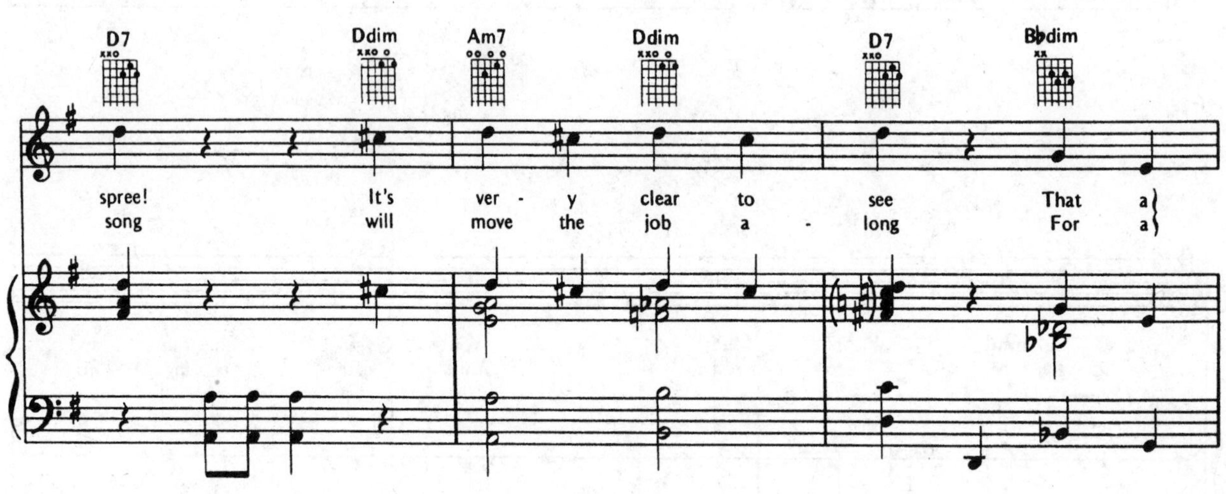
D7
Ddim
Am7
Ddim
D7
Bbdim
spree! It's ver - y clear to see That a
song will move the job a - long For a

D7
G
spoon - ful of su - gar helps the med - i - cine go

D7
Ddim
D7
Daug
down, The med - i - cine go dow - wown,
G
F♯
G
B♭dim
D7
med - i - cine go down. Just a spoon - ful of
G
Gdim
G
sug - ar helps the med - i - cine go down In a most de -
D7
1 G
B♭dim
D7
2 G
light - ful way. A rob - in way.

SPONGEBOB SQUAREPANTS THEME SONG

from SPONGEBOB SQUAREPANTS

Words and Music by MARK HARRISON, BLAISE SMITH, STEVE HILLENBURG and DEREK DRYMON

Moderately fast

C
Kids:
Painty:
Sponge - Bob Square - Pants! then drop on the deck and flop like a fish!
G
Kids: Sponge - Bob Square - Pants! All: Sponge - Bob Square - Pants!
D
Sponge - Bob Square - Pants! Sponge - Bob Square - Pants! Sponge - Bob Square -
G
N.C.
Pants!
8va

SUPERCALIFRAGILISTICEXPIALIDOCIOUS

from Walt Disney's MARY POPPINS

Words and Music by RICHARD M. SHERMAN
and ROBERT B. SHERMAN

F6
F#dim
C
C#dim
G7
C
Sup - er - cal - i - frag - il - is - tic - ex - pi - al - i - do - cious!
C
G7
C
PEARLIES
Um did - dle did - dle did - dle, um did - dle ay! Um did - dle did - dle did - dle,
mp
G7
C
Cmaj7
um did - dle ay!
BERT Be - cause I was a - fraid to speak When
MARY POPPINS He trav - eled all a - round the world And
So when the cat has got your tongue, There's
mf
C6
C#dim
G7
Dm7
G7
I was just a lad, Me fa - ther gave me nose a tweak And
ev - 'ry - where he went He'd use his word and all would say, "There
no need to dis - may. Just sum - mon up this word And then you've

Dm7 G7 C
told me I was bad. But then one day I
goes a clev - er gent!'' When dukes and ma - 'a -
got a lot to say. BERT But bet - ter use it
Cmaj7 C7 F D7
learned a word That saved me ach - in' nose, BERT and The big - gest word you
ra - jas Pass the time of day with me, MARY POPPINS I say me spe - cial
care - ful - ly Or it can change your life. PEARLIE One night I said it
G7 C
ev - er 'eard And this is 'ow it goes: Oh! 1.,2.Sup - er - cal - i -
word And then they ask me out to tea. ALL Oh! 3.Sup - er - cal - i -
to me girl And now me girl's me wife. ALL She's
Cmaj7 C6 C#dim G7 Dm7
frag - il - is - tic - ex - pi - al - i - do - cious! Ev - en though the
frag - il - is - tic - ex - pi - al - i - do - cious! Sup - er cal - i -

G7 Dm7 G7 C
sound of it is some - thing quite a - tro - cious, If you say it
frag - il - is - tic - ex - pi - al - i - do - cious! Sup - er - cal - i -
Cmaj7 C7 F F6 F♯dim
loud e - nough, you'll al - ways sound pre - co - cious. Sup - er - cal - i -
frag - il - is - tic - ex - pi - al - i - do - cious! Sup - er - cal - i -
C C♯dim G7 C 3 C
frag - il - is - tic - ex - pi - al - i - do - cious!
frag - il - is - tic - ex - pi - al - i do - cious!
F6 F♯dim C C♯dim G7 C
accel.

TAKE ME OUT TO THE BALL GAME

from TAKE ME OUT TO THE BALL GAME

Words by JACK NORWORTH
Music by ALBERT VON TILZER

G7
Cm
Buy me some pea - nuts and crack - er -
C7
jack. I don't care if I
F7
B♭
nev - er get back. Let me root, root,
F7
root for the home team. If

B♭7
F7/C
B♭7/D
E♭
G/D
they don't win it's a shame.
Cm
E♭/B♭
Adim
E♭/G
G♭7
For it's one, two,
B♭/F
B♭/D
C♯dim
B♭/D
C7
F7
three strikes, you're out at the old ball
1
B♭
F7
2
B♭
F7
B♭
game.
game.

TEN LITTLE INDIANS

Traditional

Spirited

F Gm Am B♭

mf

One lit - tle, two lit - tle, three lit - tle In - dians,
Ten lit - tle, nine lit - tle, eight lit - tle In - dians,

C Gm Am C7 F Gm

Four lit - tle, five lit - tle, six lit - tle In - dians, Seven lit - tle, eight lit - tle,
Seven lit - tle, six lit - tle, five lit - tle In - dians, Four lit - tle, three lit - tle,

Am B♭ C B♭ Am C7 F

nine lit - tle In - dians, Ten lit - tle In - dian boys.
two lit - tle In - dians, One lit - tle In - dian boy.

THERE'S A HOLE IN THE BUCKET

Traditional

Additional Lyrics

3. With what shall I fix it, dear Liza, etc.
4. With a straw, dear Henry, etc.
5. But the straw is too long, dear Liza, etc.
6. Then cut it, dear Henry, etc.
7. With what shall I cut it, dear Liza, etc.
8. With a knife, dear Henry, etc.
9. But the knife is too dull, dear Liza, etc.
10. Then sharpen it, dear Liza, etc.
11. With what shall I sharpen it, dear Liza, etc.
12. With a stone, dear Henry, etc.
13. But the stone is too dry, dear Liza, etc.
14. Then wet it, dear Henry, etc.
15. With what shall I wet it, dear Liza, etc.
16. With water, dear Henry, etc.
17. In what shall I carry it, dear Liza, etc.
18. In a bucket, dear Henry, etc.
19. There's a hole in the bucket, dear Liza, etc.

THIS LITTLE LIGHT OF MINE

Traditional

G7
C
C/G
I'm gon - na let it shine, let it shine, let it
G7
C
F
C/E
G
shine, let it shine!
C
F/C
C
F/C
C
F/C
Hide it un - der a bush - el, No!
Don't let Sa - tan (blow) it out,
Let it shine till Je - sus comes,
I'm gon - na let it
C
F
shine.
Hide it un - der a bush - el, No!
Don't let Sa - tan (blow) it out,
Let it shine till Je - sus comes,

C
C/G
I'm gon - na let it shine, let it shine, let it
G
1,2
C
G/B
Am
Cmaj7
shine, let it shine!
F
C/E
Dm7
G7
3
C
G/B
shine!
Am
Cmaj7
F
C/E
Dm7
G7
C
rit.

THIS LAND IS YOUR LAND

Words and Music by
WOODY GUTHRIE

Bright and cheerfully

G

As I went

C G

(1.) walk - ing that rib - bon of high - way I saw a -
(2.,4.,6.) your land, this land is my land, from Cal - i -
(3.) ram - bled and I fol - lowed my foot - steps to the spar - kling
(5.) shin - ing, and I was stroll - ing; the wheat fields

D D7 G

bove me that end - less sky - way; I saw be -
for - nia to the New York is - land; from the red - wood
sands of her dia - mond des - erts; while all a -
wav - ing and the dust clouds roll - ing. The fog was

C
G
low me that gold - en val - ley;
for - est to the Gulf Stream wa - ters;
round me a voice was sound - ing;
lift - ing, a voice was chant - ing:
D
D7
this land was made for you and
1-5
G
6
G
me.
2.,4.,6. This land is
3. I've roamed and
5. Well, the sun came
me.
rit.

THIS OLD MAN

Traditional

Additional Lyrics

3. This old man, he played three,
He played knick-knack on my knee.
Chorus

4. This old man, he played four,
He played knick-knack on my door.
Chorus

5. This old man, he played five,
He played knick-knack on my hive.
Chorus

6. This old man, he played six,
He played knick-knack on my sticks.
Chorus

7. This old man, he played seven,
He played knick-knack up to heaven.
Chorus

8. This old man, he played eight,
He played knick-knack at the gate.
Chorus

9. This old man, he played nine,
He played knick-knack on my line.
Chorus

10. This old man, he played ten,
He played knick-knack over again.
Chorus

A WHOLE NEW WORLD

from Walt Disney's ALADDIN

Music by ALAN MENKEN
Lyrics by TIM RICE

Em/G
F#7
F#7/A#
4fr
Bm
Bm/A
G
o - ver, side - ways and un - der on a mag - ic car - pet ride.
D
A
D
A
A7/C#
A whole new world a new fan - tas - tic point of view.
D(add9)
2fr
D
A/G
D/F#
A/G
D/F#
Bm7
2fr
E7sus
E7
3
No one to tell us no or where to go or say we're on - ly dream -
3
G/A
A
D
A
A#dim7
ing. A whole new world a daz - zling place I nev - er knew.

Bm D7/A A/G D/F# A/G D/F# Bm7 E7sus E7
But when I'm way up here it's crys - tal clear that now I'm in a
C A7sus A7 D F
whole new world with you. Un - be - liev - a - ble
B♭/D C/E Gm/B♭ A7sus A7/C#
sights in - de - scrib - a - ble feel - ing. Soar - ing, tum - bling, free -
Dm Dm/C B♭ F
wheel - ing through an end - less dia - mond sky. A whole new

C F C F
world a hun - dred thou - sand things be - gin. I'm like a
3
C/B♭ F/A C/B♭ F/A Dm7 G7sus G7
shoot - ing star I've come so far I can't go back. I'm
B♭/C C F C C♯dim7
in a whole new world with new ho - ri - zons to pur - sue.
Dm F7/C C/B♭ F/A C/B♭ F/A
3 fr
I'll chase them an - y - where. There's time to spare.

Dm7
G7sus
G7
E♭
B♭/C
C7
Dm
F/C
Let me share this whole new world with you.
A whole new
B♭(add9)
F/A
Gm7(add4)
F/A
world,
that's where we'll be.
A thrill - ing
B♭(add9)
C7sus
F
chase,
a won-d'rous place
for you and me.
rit.

THIS TRAIN

Traditional

Additional Lyrics

2. This train don't carry no gamblers, (*3 times*)
No hypocrites, no midnight ramblers,
This train is bound for glory, this train.

3. This train don't carry no liars, (*3 times*)
No hypocrites and no high flyers,
This train is bound for glory, this train.

4. This train is built for speed now, (*3 times*)
Fastest train you ever did see,
This train is bound for glory, this train.

5. This train you don't pay no transportation, (*3 times*)
No Jim Crow and no discrimination,
This train is bound for glory, this train.

6. This train don't carry no rustlers, (*3 times*)
Sidestreet walkers, two-bit hustlers,
This train is bound for glory, this train.

THREE BLIND MICE

Traditional

Brightly

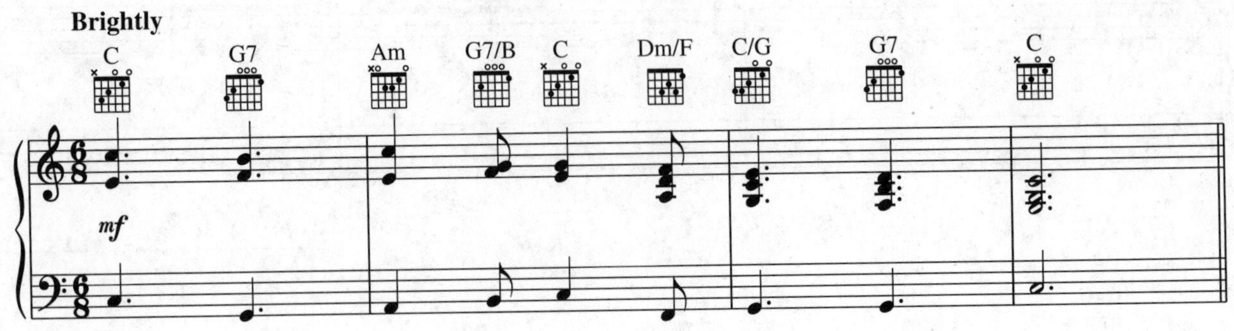

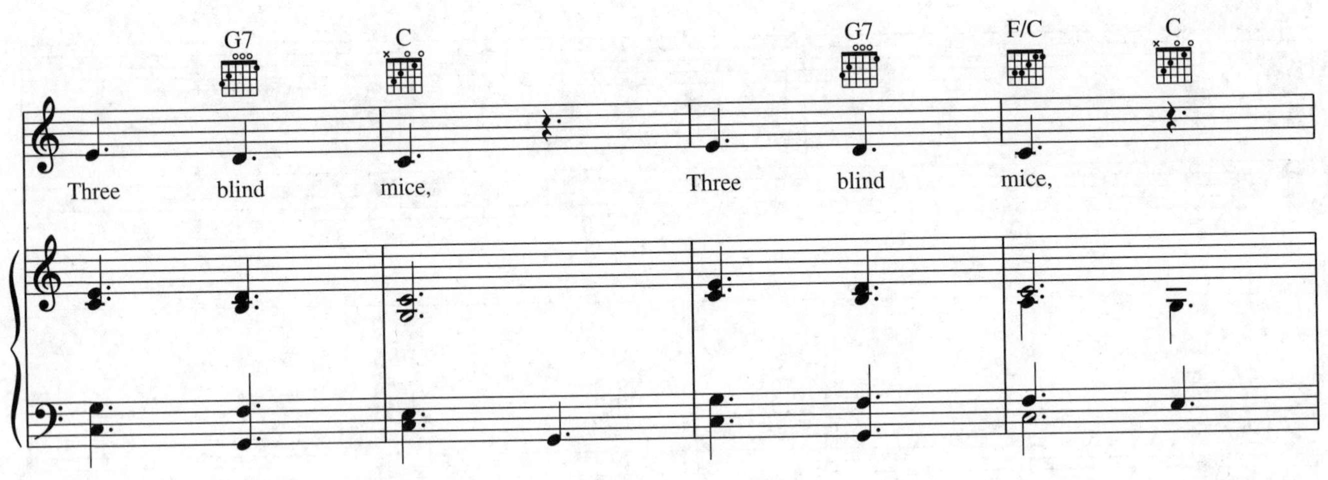

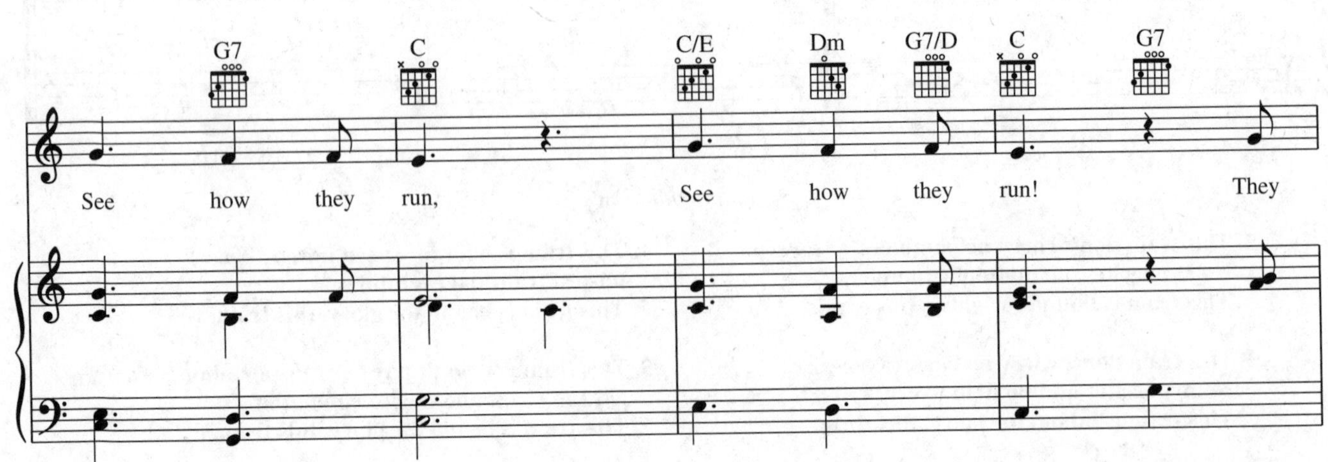

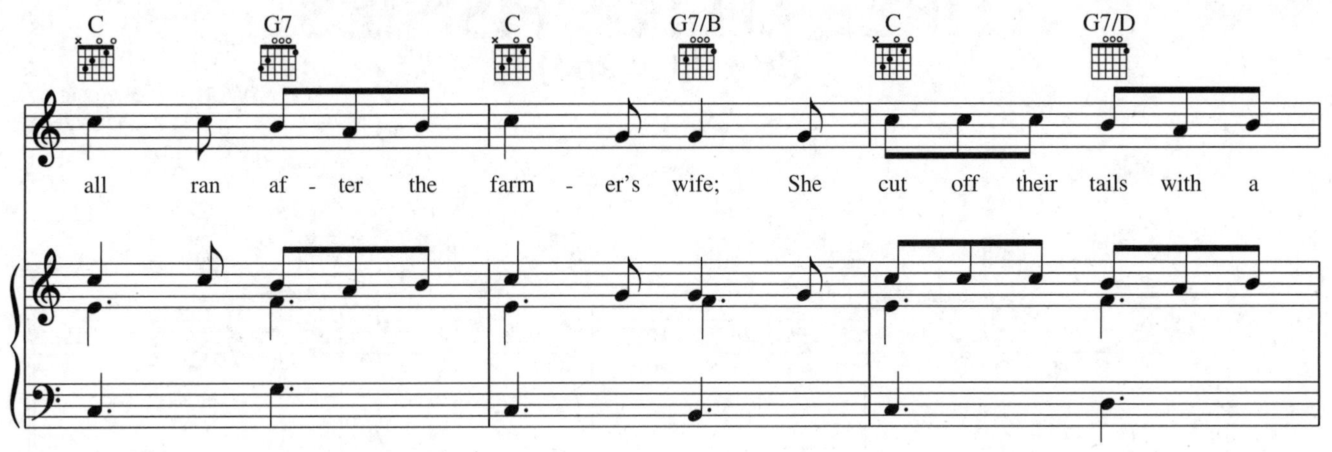
C
G7
C
G7/B
C
G7/D
all ran af - ter the farm - er's wife; She cut off their tails with a

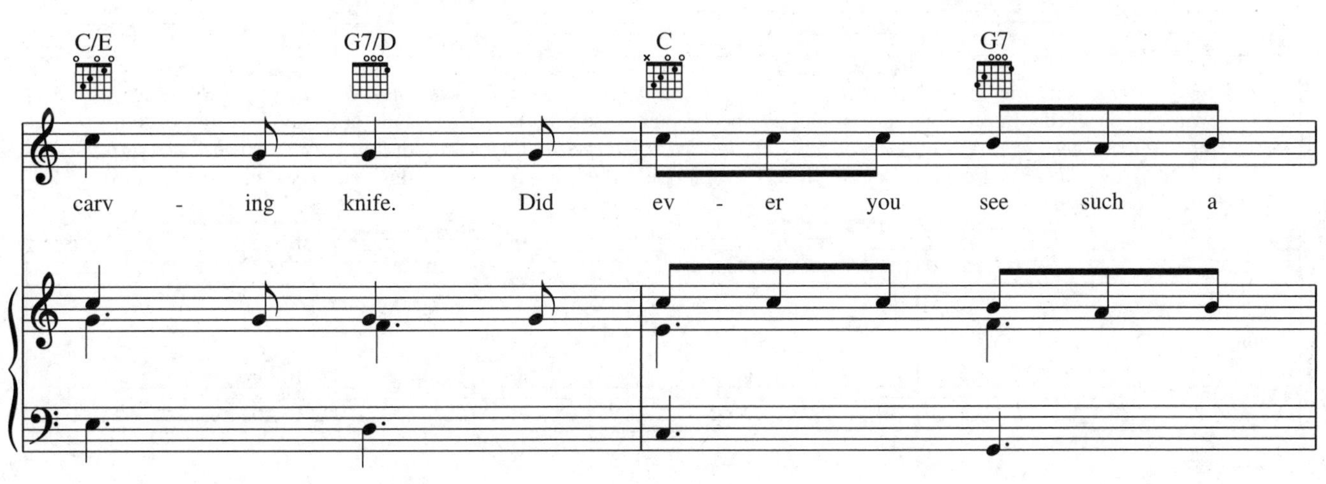
C/E
G7/D
C
G7
carv - ing knife. Did ev - er you see such a

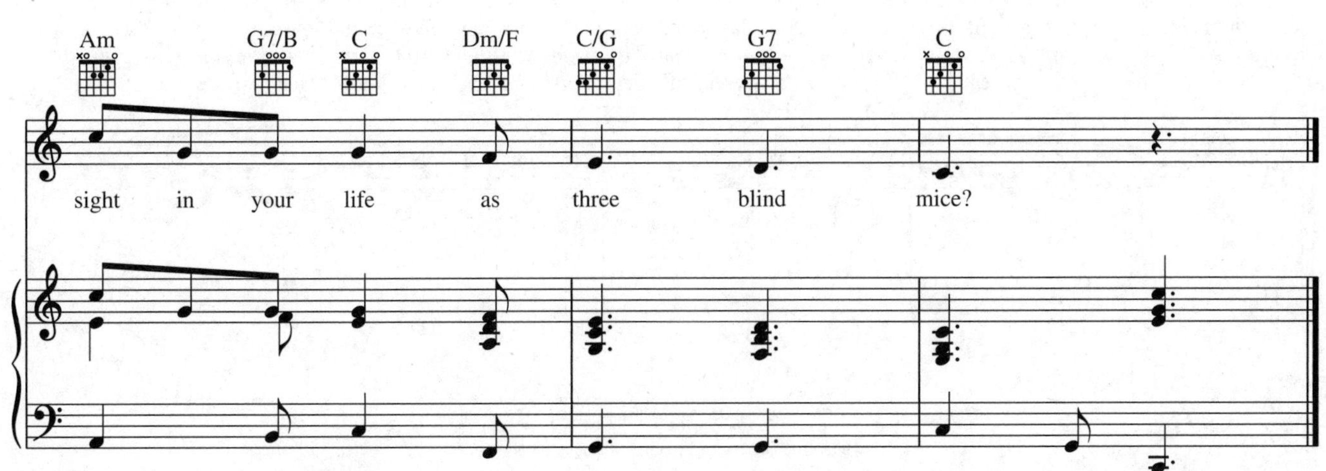
Am
G7/B
C
Dm/F
C/G
G7
C
sight in your life as three blind mice?

THREE LITTLE FISHIES
(Itty Bitty Poo)

Words and Music by
SAXIE DOWELL

Additional Lyrics

3. *"Whee!" yelled the little fishies, "Here's a lot of fun.*
We'll swim in the sea till the day is done."
They swam and they swam and it was a lark,
Till all of a sudden they met a shark!

"Whee!" 'elled de itty fitties, "Ears a wot of fun.
Ee'll fim in de fee ill de day is un."
Dey fam and dey fam and it was a wark,
Till aw of a tudden dey taw a tark!

Boop boop dittem dattem whattem. Chu!
Boop boop dittem dattem whattem. Chu!
Boop boop dittem dattem whattem. Chu!
Till aw of a tudden dey taw a tark!

4. *"Help!" cried the little fishies, "Gee! Look at all the whales!"*
And quick as they could they turned on their tails.
And back to the pool in the meadow they swam,
And they swam and they swam back over the dam.

"He'p!" tied de itty fitties, "Dee! Ook at all de fales!"
And twit as dey tood dey turned on deir tails.
And bat to de poo in de meddy dey fam,
And dey fam and dey fam bat over de dam.

Boop boop dittem dattem whattem. Chu!
Boop boop dittem dattem whattem. Chu!
Boop boop dittem dattem whattem. Chu!
And dey fam and dey fam bat over de dam.

TWINKLE, TWINKLE LITTLE STAR

Traditional

Parody

Starkle, starkle, little twink,
How I wonder what you think!
Up above the world so high,
Think you own the whole darn sky?
Starkle, starkle, little twink,
You're not so great,
That's what I think!

UNDER THE SEA

from Walt Disney's THE LITTLE MERMAID

Eb
Bb/D
Bb
F7
Just look at the world a - round you, right here on the
But fish in the bowl is luck - y, they in for a
Bb
Eb
Bb/D
Bb
o - cean floor. Such won - der - ful things sur - round you.
wors - er fate. One day when the boss get hun - gry
F7
Bb
What more is you look - in' for?
guess who gon' be on the plate.
Un - der the
Eb
Bb
F7
sea, un - der the sea.

B♭
E♭
F
Dar - lin' it's bet - ter down _ where it's wet - ter. Take _ it from
No - bod - y beat us, fry ___ us and eat us in ___ fri - ca -
B♭
B♭7
E♭
me. Up ___ on the shore they work _ all day.
see. We ___ what the land folks loves _ to cook.
F
Gm
C7
Out _ in the sun they slave _ a - way. While _ we de -
Un - der the sea we off ___ the hook. We ___ got no
E♭
F7
1
B♭
vo - tin' full - time to float - in' un - der the sea.
trou - bles life ___ is the bub - bles un - der the

F7
B♭
F7
B♭
2
E♭
B♭
F7
sea.
Un - der the
sea.
B♭
E♭
F
F7
Since__ life is sweet here
we__ got the
beat here
nat - u - ral -
B♭
B♭7
E♭
ly.
E - ven the
stur - geon an'__ the ray

F
Gm
C7
they get the urge 'n start to play. We got the
Eb
F7
Bb
spir - it, you got to hear it un - der the sea.
F7
Bb
F
Bb
The newt play the flute. The carp play the harp. The plaice
F
Bb
Eb
play the bass. And they sound - in' sharp. The bass play the brass. The chub

B♭
F
F7
B♭
play the tub. The fluke is the duke of soul. The ray
F
F7
B♭
F
F7
he can play. The lings on the strings. The trout rock - in' out. The black-
B♭
B♭/D
E♭
B♭
- fish she sings. The smelt and the sprat they know where it's at. An'
F
F7
B♭
E♭
B♭
Oh, that blow - fish blow.

F7
B♭
E♭
F7
B♭
E♭
F7
Gm
C7
E♭
F7sus
F7
B♭

F7
B♭
B♭
F7
B♭
C
G7
C
F
C/E
Un - der the sea.
Un - der the
G7
C
F
sea.
When the sar - dine be - gin the be -

G7
C
C7
guine it's mu - sic to me. What _ do they
F
G
Am
got, a lot ___ of sand. We __ got a hot crus - ta - ce - an
D7
F
G7
band. Each _ lit - tle clam here know _ how to jam ___ here un - der the
C
G7
C/E
F
sea. Each lit - tle slug here cut - tin' a

G C G7 C

rug here un - der the sea. Each lit - tle

F G Am

snail here know _ how to wail here. That's _ why it's hot - ter un - der the

D7 F G7sus G7

wa - ter. Ya _ we in luck here down _ in the muck here un - der the

C G7 C G7 C

sea. _

WHEN I'M SIXTY-FOUR

from YELLOW SUBMARINE

Words and Music by JOHN LENNON
and PAUL McCARTNEY

no chord
C
birth - day greet - ings bot - tle of wine?
If I'd been out till
C7
F
quar - ter to three
would you lock the door?
Ab7-5/Gb
C/G
A7
D9
G7/6
Will you still need me, will you still feed me when I'm six - ty
C
Am
four?
Oo

G
Am
You'll be old - er,
E
Am
too.
Ah,
Dm
and if you say the word
F
G
C
I could stay with you.

G
C
I could be hand - y
Send me a post - card,
G7
mend - ing a fuse
when your lights have gone.
drop me a line
stat - ing point of view.
no chord
You can knit a sweat - er by the fire - side,
Sun - day morn - ing
In - di - cate pre - cise - ly what you mean to say
Yours sin - cere - ly
C
go for a ride.
Do - ing the gar - den, dig - ging the weeds,
wast - ing a - way.
Give me your an - swer, fill in a form,

C7
F
Ab7-5/Gb
Who could ask for more?
Mine for - ev - er more.
Will you still need me,
Will you still need me,
C/G
A7
D9
G7/6
To Coda
C
will you still feed me,
will you still feed me,
When I'm six - ty four?
When I'm six - ty
Am
G
Ev - 'ry sum - mer we can rent a cot - tage in the Isle of Wight if it's not too dear.
Am
E
We shall scrimp and save;

Am
Dm
Grand - chil - dren on your knee;
F
G
C
Ve - ra, Chuck and Dave.
G
D.S. al Coda
CODA
C
four? Ho!
F
G7
C

WHEN THE SAINTS GO MARCHING IN

Words by KATHERINE E. PURVIS
Music by JAMES M. BLACK

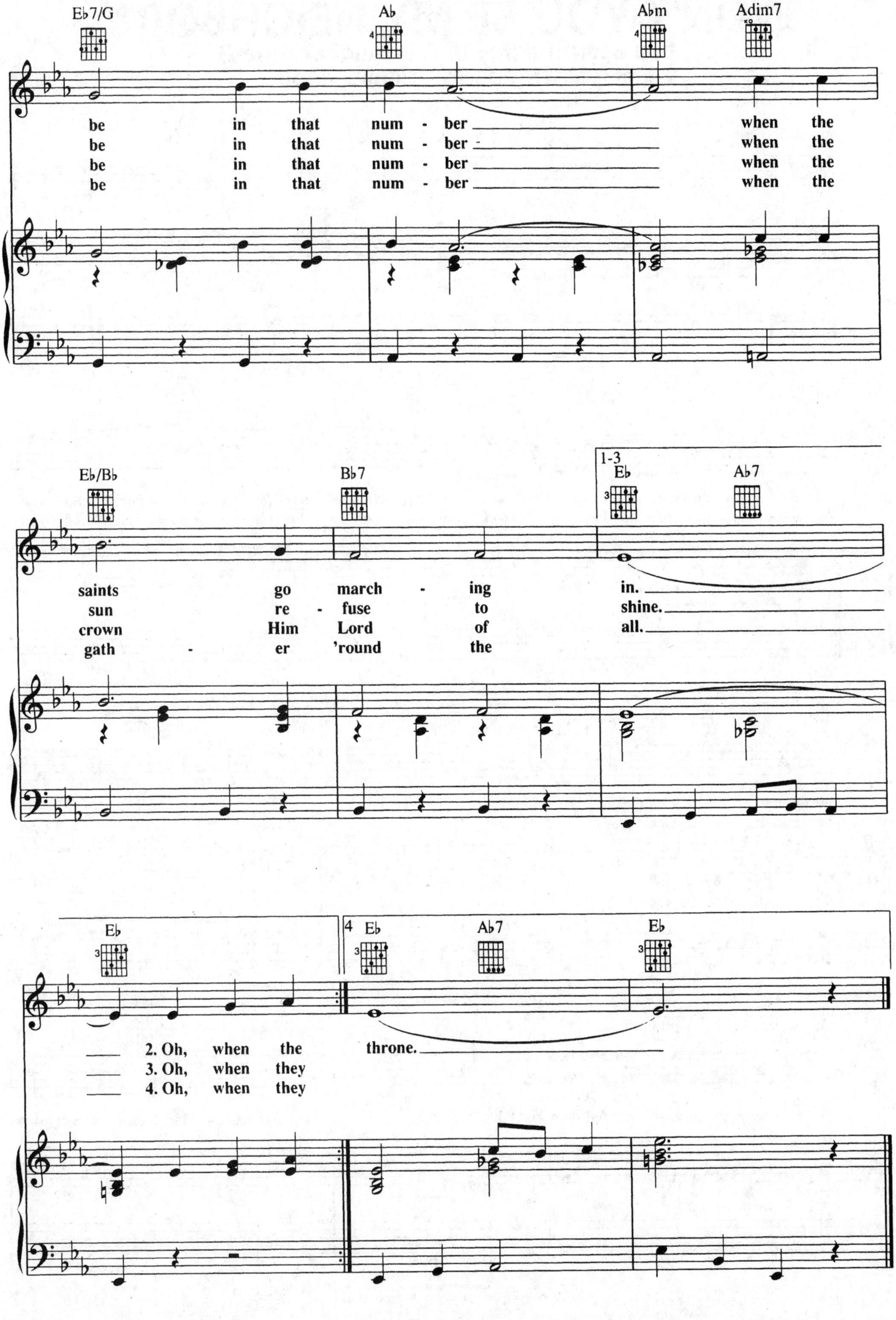

Eb7/G Ab Abm Adim7

be in that num - ber when the
be in that num - ber when the
be in that num - ber when the
be in that num - ber when the

Eb/Bb Bb7 1-3 Eb Ab7

saints go march - ing in.
sun re - fuse to shine.
crown Him Lord of all.
gath - er 'round the

Eb 4 Eb Ab7 Eb

2. Oh, when the throne.
3. Oh, when they
4. Oh, when they

WON'T YOU BE MY NEIGHBOR?
(It's a Beautiful Day in This Neighborhood)
from MISTER ROGERS' NEIGHBORHOOD

Words and Music by
FRED ROGERS

A♭m7
D♭
Gm11
C7
F6/9
Cm7
D7
hood with you. So let's make the most of this beau - ti - ful day,
Gm9
B♭m7
F
Dm7
Gm7
since we're to - geth - er we might as well say; Would you be mine? Could you be mine?
C7
F
B♭
Am7
Gm
Am7
D7
To Coda
Won't you be my neigh - bor? Won't you please, won't you please?
Gm7
C7
B♭
F
D.C. al Coda
(with repeat)
Please won't you be my neigh-bor?
CODA
Gm7
C7
B♭
F
Please won't you be my neigh-bor?

YANKEE DOODLE

Traditional

E7
A
D
called it ma - ca - ro - ni.
thick as hast - y pud - din'.
Yan - kee Doo - dle,
A
keep it up, Yan - kee Doo - dle dan - dy.
D
D♯dim
A/E
E7
Mind the mu - sic and the step and with the girls be
1
A
2
A
han - dy. han - dy. And there we saw a
There was Cap - tain

E7
A
thou - sand men as rich as Squi - re
Wash - ing - ton up - on a slap - ping
E7
A
A7
Dav - id and what they wast - ed
stal - lion, a - giv - ing or - ders
D
B7/D♯
E7
ev - 'ry day I wish it could be
to his men I guess there was a
A
D
sav - ed.
mil - lion.
Yan - kee Doo - dle, keep it up,

A
D
Yan - kee Doo - dle dan - dy. Mind the mu - sic
D♯dim
A/E
E7
1
A
and the step and with the girls be han - dy.
2
A
E7
han - dy. And then the feath - ers in his hat, they
A
E7
A
A7
looked so ver - y fine, ah I want - ed pes - ki -

D
B7/D♯
E7
ly to get to give to my Je -
A
D
mi - ma. Yan - kee Doo - dle, keep it up,
A
D
Yan - kee Doo - dle dan - dy. Mind the mu - sic
D♯dim
A/E
E7
A
and the step and with the girls be han - dy.

ZIP-A-DEE-DOO-DAH

from Walt Disney's SONG OF THE SOUTH
from Disneyland and Walt Disney World's SPLASH MOUNTAIN

Words by RAY GILBERT
Music by ALLIE WRUBEL

B♭
E♭
3fr
B♭
- shine head - in' my way.
E♭
3fr
B♭/F
Gm
3fr
E♭6
F9
B♭
Zip - a - dee - doo - dah, zip - a - dee - ay!
F7
Mis - ter Blue - bird on my
B♭dim7
B♭
Gm7
C7
shoul - der, it's the truth, it's

F
"act - ch'll" ev - 'ry - thing is "sat - is - fact - ch'll."
B♭ F7/C B♭/D B♭ Cm B♭ E♭ B♭
Zip - a-dee - doo - dah, zip - a-dee - ay!
E♭ B♭ Gm
Won - der - ful feel - ing,
C7 F7 B♭
1 B♭/D D♭dim F7/C
2
won - der - ful day!

YELLOW SUBMARINE

from YELLOW SUBMARINE

Words and Music by JOHN LENNON
and PAUL McCARTNEY

D
C
G
Em
sailed up to the sun till we
Am
Cmaj7
D
G
found the sea of green. And we
D
C
G
Em
lived be-neath the waves in our
Am
Cmaj7
D
yel - low sub - ma-rine.

Chorus:
G
D
We all live in a yel - low sub - ma-rine,
f
yel - low sub - ma-rine,
yel - low sub - ma-rine.
We all live in a
yel - low sub - ma-rine,
yel - low sub - ma-rine,
yel - low sub - ma-rine.
C
And our friends are all on
As we live a life of
mf

G
Em
Am
Cmaj7
board, man - y more of them live next
ease, ev - 'ry one of us has all we
D
G
D
C
door. And the band be - gins to
need. Sky of blue and sea of
1
G
3
play:
2
G
Em
Am
Cmaj7
D
D.S. and Fade
green in our yel - low sub - ma - rine.

YOU'VE GOT A FRIEND IN ME

from Walt Disney's TOY STORY

from Walt Disney Pictures' TOY STORY 2 - A Pixar Film

Music and Lyrics by
RANDY NEWMAN

Ab
Eb/G
G7
Cm
and miles from your nice warm bed,
There is - n't an - y - thing I would - n't do for you.
Ab
D/A
Eb/Bb
G/B
Cm
Ab7
G
Cm
F7
Bb7
you just re-mem-ber what your old pal said. Son, you've got a friend in me.
If we stick to-geth-er we can see it through, 'cause you've got a friend in me.
Eb
C7
F7
Bb7
1
Eb
G7/D
Yeah, you've got a friend in me.
Yeah, you've got a friend in me.
3
Cm
B7
Eb/Bb
Ebdim/Bb
Bb7

2
Eb
Ebmaj7
Eb7
Ab
D
Now, some oth - er folks might be a lit - tle bit smart - er than I am,
Eb6
D7
Eb6
D
Em7
big - ger and strong - er too. May - be. But none of them will
Fdim7
D/F#
Gm
C7
Fm
Bb7
ev - er love you the way I do, just me and you, boy.
Eb
Bb7#5
Eb7
Ab
Adim7
And as the years go by, our friend - ship will nev - er die.

Eb/Bb
Eb
Ab
Adim7
Eb/Bb
G7/B
Cm
You're gon - na see it's our des - ti - ny.
molto rit.
F7
Bb7
Eb
C7
F7
Bb7
You've got a friend in me.
You've got a friend in me.
a tempo
Eb
C7
F7
Bb7
Eb
G7/D
You've got a friend in me.
Cm
B7
Eb/Bb
Ebdim/Bb
Bb7
Eb
rit.

THE BEST EVER COLLECTION

ARRANGED FOR PIANO, VOICE AND GUITAR

150 of the Most Beautiful Songs Ever
150 ballads
00360735 .... $27.00

150 More of the Most Beautiful Songs Ever
150 songs
00311318 .... $29.99

More of the Best Acoustic Rock Songs Ever
69 tunes
00311738 .... $19.95

Best Acoustic Rock Songs Ever
65 acoustic hits
00310984 .... $19.95

Best Big Band Songs Ever
68 big band hits
00359129 .... $17.99

Best Blues Songs Ever
73 blues tunes
00312874 .... $19.99

Best Broadway Songs Ever
83 songs
00309155 .... $24.99

More of the Best Broadway Songs Ever
82 songs
00311501 .... $22.95

Best Children's Songs Ever
96 songs
00310358 .... $19.99

Best Christmas Songs Ever
69 holiday favorites
00359130 .... $24.99

Best Classic Rock Songs Ever
64 hits
00310800 .... $22.99

Best Classical Music Ever
86 classical favorites
00310674 (Piano Solo) $19.95

The Best Country Rock Songs Ever
52 hits
00118881 .... $19.99

Best Country Songs Ever
78 classic country hits
00359135 .... $19.99

Best Disco Songs Ever
50 songs
00312565 .... $19.99

Best Dixieland Songs Ever
90 songs
00312326 .... $19.99

Best Early Rock 'n' Roll Songs Ever
74 songs
00310816 .... $19.95

Best Easy Listening Songs Ever
75 mellow favorites
00359193 .... $19.95

Best Gospel Songs Ever
80 gospel songs
00310503 .... $19.99

Best Hymns Ever
118 hymns
00310774 .... $18.99

Best Jazz Standards Ever
77 jazz hits
00311641 .... $19.95

More of the Best Jazz Standards Ever
74 beloved jazz hits
00311023 .... $19.95

Best Latin Songs Ever
67 songs
00310355 .... $19.99

Best Love Songs Ever
65 favorite love songs
00359198 .... $19.95

Best Movie Songs Ever
71 songs
00310063 .... $19.99

Best Praise & Worship Songs Ever
80 all-time favorites
00311057 .... $22.99

More of the Best Praise & Worship Songs Ever
76 songs
00311800 .... $24.99

Best R&B Songs Ever
66 songs
00310184 .... $19.95

Best Rock Songs Ever
63 songs
00490424 .... $18.95

Best Songs Ever
72 must-own classics
00359224 .... $24.99

Best Soul Songs Ever
70 hits
00311427 .... $19.95

Best Standards Ever, Vol. 1 (A-L)
72 beautiful ballads
00359231 .... $17.95

Best Standards Ever, Vol. 2 (M-Z)
73 songs
00359232 .... $17.99

More of the Best Standards Ever, Vol. 1 (A-L)
76 all-time favorites
00310813 .... $17.95

More of the Best Standards Ever, Vol. 2 (M-Z)
75 stunning standards
00310814 .... $17.95

Best Torch Songs Ever
70 sad and sultry favorites
00311027 .... $19.95

Best Wedding Songs Ever
70 songs
00311096 .... $19.95

Prices, contents and availability subject to change without notice. Not all products available outside the U.S.A.

HAL•LEONARD® CORPORATION
7777 W. BLUEMOUND RD. P.O. BOX 13819 MILWAUKEE, WI 53213

Visit us online for complete songlists at
www.halleonard.com

THE GRAMMY AWARDS®

SONGBOOKS FROM HAL LEONARD

These elite collections of the nominees and winners of Grammy Awards since the honor's inception in 1958 provide a snapshot of the changing times in popular music.

PIANO/VOCAL/GUITAR

GRAMMY AWARDS RECORD OF THE YEAR 1958–2011

Beat It • Beautiful Day • Bridge over Troubled Water • Don't Know Why • Don't Worry, Be Happy • The Girl from Ipanema (Garôta De Ipanema) • Hotel California • I Will Always Love You • Just the Way You Are • Mack the Knife • Moon River • My Heart Will Go on (Love Theme from 'Titanic') • Rehab • Sailing • Unforgettable • Up, Up and Away • The Wind Beneath My Wings • and more.

00313603 P/V/G.......$19.99

THE GRAMMY AWARDS SONG OF THE YEAR 1958–1969

Battle of New Orleans • Born Free • Fever • The Good Life • A Hard Day's Night • Harper Valley P.T.A. • Hello, Dolly! • Hey Jude • King of the Road • Little Green Apples • Mrs. Robinson • Ode to Billy Joe • People • Somewhere, My Love • Strangers in the Night • A Time for Us (Love Theme) • Volare • Witchcraft • Yesterday • and more.

00313598 P/V/G.......$19.99

THE GRAMMY AWARDS SONG OF THE YEAR 1970–1979

Alone Again (Naturally) • American Pie • At Seventeen • Don't It Make My Brown Eyes Blue • Honesty • (I Never Promised You A) Rose Garden • I Write the Songs • Killing Me Softly with His Song • Let It Be • Me and Bobby McGee • Send in the Clowns • Song Sung Blue • Stayin' Alive • Three Times a Lady • The Way We Were • You're So Vain • You've Got a Friend • and more.

00313599 P/V/G.......$19.99

THE GRAMMY AWARDS SONG OF THE YEAR 1980–1989

Against All Odds (Take a Look at Me Now) • Always on My Mind • Beat It • Bette Davis Eyes • Don't Worry, Be Happy • Ebony and Ivory • Endless Love • Every Breath You Take • Eye of the Tiger • Fame • Fast Car • Hello • I Just Called to Say I Love You • La Bamba • Nine to Five • The Rose • Somewhere Out There • Time After Time • We Are the World • and more.

00313600 P/V/G.......$19.99

THE GRAMMY AWARDS SONG OF THE YEAR 1990–1999

Can You Feel the Love Tonight • (Everything I Do) I Do It for You • From a Distance • Give Me One Reason • I Swear • Kiss from a Rose • Losing My Religion • My Heart Will Go on (Love Theme from 'Titanic') • Nothing Compares 2 U • Smooth • Streets of Philadelphia • Tears in Heaven • Unforgettable • Walking in Memphis • A Whole New World • You Oughta Know • and more.

00313601 P/V/G.......$19.99

THE GRAMMY AWARDS SONG OF THE YEAR 2000–2009

Beautiful • Beautiful Day • Breathe • Chasing Pavements • Complicated • Dance with My Father • Daughters • Don't Know Why • Fallin' • I Hope You Dance • I'm Yours • Live like You Were Dying • Poker Face • Rehab • Single Ladies (Put a Ring on It) • A Thousand Miles • Umbrella • Use Somebody • Viva La Vida • and more.

00313602 P/V/G.......$19.99

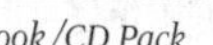

THE GRAMMY AWARDS BEST COUNTRY SONG 1964–2011

Always on My Mind • Before He Cheats • Behind Closed Doors • Bless the Broken Road • Butterfly Kisses • Dang Me • Forever and Ever, Amen • The Gambler • I Still Believe in You • I Swear • King of the Road • Live like You Were Dying • Love Can Build a Bridge • Need You Now • On the Road Again • White Horse • You Decorated My Life • and more.

00313604 P/V/G.......$19.99

THE GRAMMY AWARDS BEST R&B SONG 1958–2011

After the Love Has Gone • Ain't No Sunshine • Be Without You • Billie Jean • End of the Road • Good Golly Miss Molly • Hit the Road Jack • If You Don't Know Me by Now • Papa's Got a Brand New Bag • Respect • Shine • Single Ladies (Put a Ring on It) • (Sittin' On) the Dock of the Bay • Superstition • U Can't Touch This • We Belong Together • and more.

00313605 P/V/G.......$19.99

THE GRAMMY AWARDS BEST POP & ROCK GOSPEL ALBUMS (2000–2011)

Call My Name • Come on Back to Me • Deeper Walk • Forever • Gone • I Need You • I Smile • I Will Follow • King • Leaving 99 • Lifesong • Looking Back at You • Much of You • My Love Remains • Say So • Somebody's Watching • Step by Step/Forever We Will Sing • Tunnel • Unforgetful You • You Hold My World • Your Love Is a Song • and more.

00313680 P/V/G.......$16.99

ELECTRONIC KEYBOARD

THE GRAMMY AWARDS RECORD OF THE YEAR 1958-2011 – VOL. 160

All I Wanna Do • Bridge over Troubled Water • Don't Know Why • The Girl from Ipanema (Garôta De Ipanema) • Hotel California • I Will Always Love You • Just the Way You Are • Killing Me Softly with His Song • Love Will Keep Us Together • Rehab • Unforgettable • What's Love Got to Do with It • The Wind Beneath My Wings • and more.

00100315 E-Z Play Today #160.......$16.99

PRO VOCAL

WOMEN'S EDITIONS

THE GRAMMY AWARDS BEST FEMALE POP VOCAL PERFORMANCE 1990-1999 — VOL. 57

Book/CD Pack

All I Wanna Do • Building a Mystery • Constant Craving • I Will Always Love You • I Will Remember You • My Heart Will Go on (Love Theme from 'Titanic') • No More "I Love You's" • Something to Talk About (Let's Give Them Something to Talk About) • Unbreak My Heart • Vision of Love.

00740446 Melody/Lyrics/Chords.......$14.99

THE GRAMMY AWARDS BEST FEMALE POP VOCAL PERFORMANCE 2000-2009 – VOL. 58

Book/CD Pack

Ain't No Other Man • Beautiful • Chasing Pavements • Don't Know Why • Halo • I Try • I'm like a Bird • Rehab • Since U Been Gone • Sunrise.

00740447 Melody/Lyrics/Chords.......$14.99

MEN'S EDITIONS

THE GRAMMY AWARDS BEST MALE POP VOCAL PERFORMANCE 1990-1999 – VOL. 59

Book/CD Pack

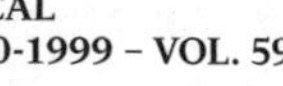

Brand New Day • Can You Feel the Love Tonight • Candle in the Wind 1997 • Change the World • If I Ever Lose My Faith in You • Kiss from a Rose • My Father's Eyes • Oh, Pretty Woman • Tears in Heaven • When a Man Loves a Woman.

00740448 Melody/Lyrics/Chords.......$14.99

THE GRAMMY AWARDS BEST MALE POP VOCAL PERFORMANCE 2000-2009 – VOL. 60

Book/CD Pack

Cry Me a River • Daughters • Don't Let Me Be Lonely Tonight • Make It Mine • Say • Waiting on the World to Change • What Goes Around...Comes Around Interlude • Your Body Is a Wonderland.

00740449 Melody/Lyrics/Chords.......$14.99

Prices, contents, and availabilbity subject to change without notice.

7777 W. Bluemound Rd. P.O. Box 13819 Milwaukee, WI 53213

www.halleonard.com

0713

Play the best songs from the Roaring '20s to today!

Each collection features dozens of the most memorable songs of each decade, or in your favorite musical style, arranged in piano/vocal/guitar format.

THE 1920s

Over 100 songs that shaped the decade: Ain't We Got Fun? • Basin Street Blues • Bye Bye Blackbird • Can't Help Lovin' Dat Man • I Wanna Be Loved by You • Makin' Whoopee • Ol' Man River • Puttin' On the Ritz • Toot, Toot, Tootsie • Yes Sir, That's My Baby • and more.
00311200..$24.95

THE 1930s

97 essential songs from the 1930s: April in Paris • Body and Soul • Cheek to Cheek • Falling in Love with Love • Georgia on My Mind • Heart and Soul • I'll Be Seeing You • The Lady Is a Tramp • Mood Indigo • My Funny Valentine • You Are My Sunshine • and more.
00311193..$24.95

THE 1940s

An amazing collection of over 100 songs from the '40s: Boogie Woogie Bugle Boy • Don't Get Around Much Anymore • Have I Told You Lately That I Love You • I'll Remember April • Route 66 • Sentimental Journey • Take the "A" Train • You'd Be So Nice to Come Home To • and more.
00311192..$24.95

THE 1950s

Over 100 pivotal songs from the 1950s, including: All Shook Up • Bye Bye Love • Chantilly Lace • Fever • Great Balls of Fire • Kansas City • Love and Marriage • Mister Sandman • Rock Around the Clock • Sixteen Tons • Tennessee Waltz • Wonderful! Wonderful! • and more.
00311191..$24.95

THE 1960s

104 '60s essentials, including: Baby Love • California Girls • Dancing in the Street • Hey Jude • I Heard It Through the Grapevine • Respect • Stand by Me • Twist and Shout • Will You Love Me Tomorrow • Yesterday • You Keep Me Hangin' On • and more.
00311190..$24.95

THE 1970s

Over 80 of the best songs from the '70s: American Pie • Band on the Run • Come Sail Away • Dust in the Wind • I Feel the Earth Move • Let It Be • Morning Has Broken • Smoke on the Water • Take a Chance on Me • The Way We Were • You're So Vain • and more.
00311189..$24.95

THE 1980s

Over 70 classics from the age of power pop and hair metal: Against All Odds • Call Me • Ebony and Ivory • The Heat Is On • Jump • Manic Monday • Sister Christian • Time After Time • Up Where We Belong • What's Love Got to Do with It • and more.
00311188 ....$24.95

THE 2000s

59 of the best songs that brought in the new millennium: Accidentally in Love • Beautiful • Don't Know Why • Get the Party Started • Hey Ya! • I Hope You Dance • 1985 • This Love • A Thousand Miles • Wherever You Will Go • Who Let the Dogs Out • You Raise Me Up • and more.
00311186..$24.95

ACOUSTIC ROCK

Over 70 songs, including: About a Girl • Barely Breathing • Blowin' in the Wind • Fast Car • Landslide • Turn! Turn! Turn! (To Everything There Is a Season) • Walk on the Wild Side • and more.
00311747..$24.95

THE BEATLES

Over 90 of the finest from this extraordinary band: All My Loving • Back in the U.S.S.R. • Blackbird • Come Together • Get Back • Help! • Hey Jude • If I Fell • Let It Be • Michelle • Penny Lane • Something • Twist and Shout • Yesterday • more!
00311389..$29.99

BROADWAY – 2ND EDITION

Over 90 songs of the stage: Any Dream Will Do • Blue Skies • Cabaret • Don't Cry for Me, Argentina • Edelweiss • Hello, Dolly! • I'll Be Seeing You • Memory • The Music of the Night • Oklahoma • Summer Nights • There's No Business Like Show Business • Tomorrow • more.
00311222..$24.99

CHILDREN'S SONGS

Over 110 songs, including: Bob the Builder "Intro Theme Song" • "C" Is for Cookie • Eensy Weensy Spider • I'm Popeye the Sailor Man • The Muppet Show Theme • Old MacDonald • Sesame Street Theme • and more.
00311823..$24.99

CHRISTMAS

Over 100 essential holiday favorites: Blue Christmas • The Christmas Song • Deck the Hall • Frosty the Snow Man • Joy to the World • Merry Christmas, Darling • Rudolph the Red-Nosed Reindeer • Silver Bells • and more!
00311241..$24.95

COUNTRY

96 essential country standards, including: Achy Breaky Heart • Crazy • The Devil Went down to Georgia • Elvira • Friends in Low Places • God Bless the U.S.A. • Here You Come Again • Lucille • Redneck Woman • Tennessee Waltz • and more.
00311296..$24.95

Complete contents listings are available online at **www.halleonard.com**

LOVE SONGS

Over 80 romantic hits: Can You Feel the Love Tonight • Endless Love • From This Moment On • Have I Told You Lately • I Just Called to Say I Love You • Love Will Keep Us Together • My Heart Will Go On • Wonderful Tonight • You Are So Beautiful • more.
00311235..$24.95

LOVE STANDARDS

100 romantic standards: Dream a Little Dream of Me • The Glory of Love • I Left My Heart in San Francisco • I've Got My Love to Keep Me Warm • The Look of Love • A Time for Us • You Are the Sunshine of My Life • and more.
00311256..$24.95

MOVIE SONGS

94 of the most popular silver screen songs: Alfie • Beauty and the Beast • Chariots of Fire • Footloose • I Will Remember You • Jailhouse Rock • Moon River • People • Somewhere Out There • Summer Nights • Unchained Melody • and more.
00311236..$24.95

ROCK

Over 80 essential rock classics: Black Magic Woman • Day Tripper • Free Bird • A Groovy Kind of Love • I Shot the Sheriff • The Joker • My Sharona • Oh, Pretty Woman • Proud Mary • Rocket Man • Roxanne • Takin' Care of Business • A Whiter Shade of Pale • Wild Thing • more!
00311390..$24.95

TV SONGS

Over 100 terrific tube tunes, including: The Addams Family Theme • Bonanza • The Brady Bunch • Desperate Housewives Main Title • I Love Lucy • Law and Order • Linus and Lucy • Sesame Street Theme • Theme from the Simpsons • Theme from the X-Files • and more!
00311223..$24.95

WEDDING

83 songs of love and devotion: All I Ask of You • Canon in D • Don't Know Much • Here, There and Everywhere • Love Me Tender • My Heart Will Go On • Somewhere Out There • Wedding March • You Raise Me Up • and more.
00311309..$24.95

For More Information, See Your Local Music Dealer, Or Write To:

7777 W. Bluemound Rd. P.O. Box 13819 Milwaukee, WI 53213

Prices, contents and availability subject to change without notice.

0913